MY FACTFILE!

FILL IN YOUR FOOTY DETAILS!

MY NAME IS . . .

MY FAVOURITE FOOTBALL TEAM IS . . .

MY FAVOURITE PLAYER IS . . .

THE POSITION I PLAY IN IS . . .

THE TEAMS I PLAY FOR ARE . . .

MY FAVOURITE FOOTBALL BOOTS ARE . . .

D1589112

7 0

CHECK OUT THESE OTHER MATCH! TITLES FROM MACMILLAN!

MATCH! PUZZLE BOOK

MATCH! FOOTBALL RECORDS BOOK

MATCH! JOKE BOOK

MATCH! ENGLAND HEROES BOOK

MATCH! ANNUAL 2021

MATCH! FUN BOOK

TO ORDER, GO TO: WWW.PANMACMILLAN.COM

MATCH!

FOOTBALL STARS!

MACMILLAN CHILDREN'S BOOKS

First published 2020 by Macmillan Children's Books
an imprint of Pan Macmillan
The Smithson, 6 Briset Street, London, EC1M 5NR
Associated companies throughout the world
www.panmacmillan.com

ISBN 978-1-5290-2664-1

Text copyright © Kelsey Media 2020
Photos copyright © Getty Images

All rights reserved. No part of this publication may be reproduced,
stored in a retrieval system, or transmitted, in any form or by any
means (electronic, mechanical, photocopying, recording or otherwise),
without the prior written permission of the publisher.

Pan Macmillan does not have any control over, or any responsibility
for, any author or third party websites referred to in or on this book.

1 3 5 7 9 8 6 4 2

A CIP catalogue record for this book
is available from the British Library.

Written by Chris Hunt
Edited by Stephen Fishlock
Designed by Darryl Tooth
Stats correct up to March, 2020.

Printed and bound by CPI Group (UK) Ltd, Croydon CR0 4YY

This book is sold subject to the condition that it shall not,
by way of trade or otherwise, be lent, resold, hired out,
or otherwise circulated without the publisher's prior consent
in any form of binding or cover other than that in which
it is published and without a similar condition including this
condition being imposed on the subsequent purchaser.

CONTENTS!

FORWARDS

FORWARDS QUIZ

MIDFIELDERS & WINGERS

MIDFIELDERS & WINGERS QUIZ

DEFENDERS & GOALKEEPERS

DEFENDERS & GOALKEEPERS QUIZ

WOMEN'S FOOTBALL

WOMEN'S FOOTBALL QUIZ

MY TOP 10

FORWARDS

LIONEL
MESSI

Forward

Club: Barcelona

DOB: 24/06/1987

Place of Birth: Rosario, Argentina

Transfer Value: £150 million

Strongest Foot: Left

Country: Argentina

International Debut: 17/08/2005 v Hungary

International Caps: 138

International Goals: 70

Top Skill: High-speed dribbling

One of the most awesome players ever, Messi is also one of the game's greatest goal scorers. A one-club player, he has spent his whole career with Barcelona. He was just 13 when his dad moved the family from Argentina to Spain so Leo could sign for the club's youth academy. And in the 19 years since, he has rewritten the record books and has amazed footy fans with his fancy feet, his driving runs and his ability to dink the ball over opposition goalkeepers. He is the top scorer in the history of the Spanish league, more than 100 goals ahead of his nearest rival, but his international career has been a different story. He was red carded on his Argentina debut after just 43 seconds in 2005, and although he captained his country to second place at the 2014 World Cup, he hasn't really achieved the same level of success with Argentina as he has in club footy.

HIS GAME RATED!

✓ He's one of the world's best dribblers and has lightning-quick feet!

✓ He's a match winner and scores vital goals when it really counts!

✗ He's a bit on the short side, which limits his threat in the air!

PLAYER STATS

PACE
92

POWER
65

SHOOTING
95

DEFENDING
50

HEADERS
66

SKILL
97

MATCH! 11

STAT ATTACK!

DID YOU KNOW?

Messi scored his first Barca hat-trick in 2007 against deadly rivals Real Madrid!

73

He was on red-hot form in 2011-12, scoring 73 in all comps and breaking the world record for goals in one season.

6

Leo has been Europe's top goal scorer a record six times. No one has won the Golden Shoe more. Top man!

10

Messi won his tenth La Liga title in 2019. That's more than any other Barca player.

8

With eight hat-tricks in the Champions League, only Ronaldo has scored as many as Lionel Messi.

HARRY KANE

Striker

Club: Tottenham	**Country:** England
DOB: 28/07/1993	**International Debut:** 27/03/2015 v Lithuania
Place of Birth: London, England	**International Caps:** 45
Transfer Value: £135 million	**International Goals:** 32
Strongest Foot: Right	**Top Skill:** Finishing

Harry Kane is one of England's true world-class players and he's an outstanding captain of the national team. He led the Three Lions to the semi-finals of the 2018 World Cup and finished the tournament as top scorer, becoming the first English player to do this since Gary Lineker in 1986. He even hit a hat-trick at the finals against Panama. A class act, he bangs them in from close range and from outside the box, with either foot or with his head.

He really is the scorer of some amazing goals – and loads of them too. He's won the Premier League Golden Boot twice and is already Tottenham's third highest goal scorer ever and England's sixth highest. Early in his career he was loaned out to clubs like Leyton Orient, Millwall and Norwich, but these days he's more likely to be linked to big-money moves abroad. He'll probably stay at Spurs though – after all, he is one of their own!

HIS GAME RATED!

 He's on course to become England's greatest ever goal scorer!

There's more to his game than goals and his hold up play is excellent!

 His goals are amazing but he's not really the quickest of strikers!

PLAYER STATS

PACE
70

POWER
86

SHOOTING
95

DEFENDING
53

HEADERS
88

SKILL
82

DID YOU KNOW?

Harry Kane scored his first England goal just 79 seconds into his international debut against Lithuania!

STAT ATTACK!

It took the Spurs super striker just 141 games to score his first 100 Prem goals. Only Alan Shearer has done it quicker.

The England star grabbed 12 goals in eight games in the Euro 2020 qualifiers, which made him overall top scorer!

Harry wore the number 37 shirt when he made his Spurs debut against Hearts in the Europa League in August 2011.

When he won his second Prem Golden Boot in 2016-17, Kane scored 29 goals in just 30 games. What a hot shot!

Harry holds the Premier League record for the most goals in a calendar year. He scored an epic 39 in 2017, breaking Alan Shearer's 22-year-old record.

ROBERT LEWANDOWSKI

Striker

Club: Bayern Munich	**Country:** Poland
DOB: 21/08/1988	**International Debut:** 10/09/2008 v San Marino
Place of Birth: Warsaw, Poland	**International Caps:** 112
Transfer Value: £55 million	**International Goals:** 61
Strongest Foot: Right	**Top Skill:** Positioning

A deadly marksman inside the box, Robert Lewandowski is strong in the air and great at finishing first time. He is Poland's captain and the country's biggest star by far. The towering striker is also a legend at Bayern Munich, but it was with big rivals Borussia Dortmund that he first became a mega star. He won two Bundesliga titles and his first German Golden Boot with the club. But after signing for Bayern Munich in 2014, Lewa won five more league titles and finished top scorer a further three times. He scored over 40 goals in all comps for four seasons in a row for Bayern and he's currently ranked third highest goal scorer in German league history. He's been almost as prolific in the Champions League too and in 2019 he set a new competition speed scoring record by notching four against Red Star Belgrade in just 14 minutes and 32 seconds. What a hero!

HIS GAME RATED!

✓ Lewa's a strong centre-forward who can out-muscle any defence!

✓ He's one of the top scorers in the history of the Champions League!

✗ He's not the best with his left foot but he's great with his right!

PLAYER STATS

PACE
75

POWER
86

SHOOTING
88

DEFENDING
52

HEADERS
82

SKILL
85

STAT ATTACK!

The Bayern mega star scored five in nine minutes after coming on as a sub against Wolfsburg in 2015. No one has hit five goals faster.

5

16

He scored 16 goals to help Poland get to the 2018 World Cup, making him the top scorer in qualification.

Lewa is just goal crazy. Up to 2019, he had finished the German league season as top scorer four times.

4

DID YOU KNOW?

Lewa was born to be a footballer. His dad played football in the Polish second division!

13

He equalled a competition record when he scored 13 goals as Poland reached the finals of Euro 2016.

CRISTIANO RONALDO

Forward

Club: Juventus	**Country:** Portugal
DOB: 05/02/1985	**International Debut:** 20/08/2003 v Kazakhstan
Place of Birth: Funchal, Madeira, Portugal	**International Caps:** 164
Transfer Value: £80 million	**International Goals:** 99
Strongest Foot: Right	**Top Skill:** Finishing

Cristiano Ronaldo is such a mega athlete that he's won almost everything there is to win in the game, for both club and country. The biggest Champions League star of them all, he's lifted the famous trophy a total of five times in his career and he's scored more goals in the comp than anyone else, as well as more headed goals and more penalties. As captain of Portugal, he led the team to glory at Euro 2016, despite being forced off the pitch through injury after just 25 minutes of the final. He's also scored more international goals than just about everyone else in the history of the game. Well known for his spectacular strikes, devastating free-kicks, powerful running and acrobatic overhead kicks, he's been a success wherever he's played – he's won the Premier League in England, La Liga in Spain and Serie A in Italy. That pretty much makes him a superstar!

HIS GAME RATED!

✓ Awesome at scoring from distance, he's a sick free-kick specialist too!

✓ He's powerful in the air and great at timing runs to outjump defenders!

✗ He's a goal machine but his defending really isn't up to much.

PLAYER STATS

PACE
90

POWER
91

SHOOTING
95

DEFENDING
52

HEADERS
94

SKILL
92

MATCH! 23

DID YOU KNOW?
Ronaldo has a museum dedicated to his career. It's where he keeps all his trophies and medals!

STAT ATTACK!

21

He holds the record for the most European Championship matches played, winning the 2016 final in his 21st game. That's mega!

Ron bagged 61 goals in all comps in the 2014-15 season – that's still a Real Madrid record.

61

4

Ron has scored four Champions League final goals. That's more than anyone else!

In 2013-14 he scored the highest number of goals in a single Champions League season. His goal in the final was his 17th of the campaign!

17

450

The total number of goals he scored for Real Madrid is 450. That's still a club record!

NEYMAR

Forward

Club: Paris Saint-Germain	**Country:** Brazil
DOB: 05/02/1992	**International Debut:** 10/08/2010 v USA
Place of Birth: Mogi das Cruzes, Brazil	**International Caps:** 101
Transfer Value: £162 million	**International Goals:** 61
Strongest Foot: Right	**Top Skill:** Speedy dribbling

One of the flashiest superstars in world football, Neymar scored against the USA on his Brazil debut in 2010, aged just 18. West Ham and Chelsea both made multi-million pound bids to sign him, but footy legend Pele persuaded him to stay in Brazil. He finally moved to Europe three years later, when he signed for Barcelona and forged the sick 'MSN' strike force with Suarez and Messi. He scored in the Champions League final in 2015 as Barca beat Juventus to complete the 'treble'. He notched 39 goals that season – 10 in the Champions League, which made him the joint highest scorer in the comp. In 2017 Paris Saint-Germain smashed the world transfer record to sign him, paying a whopping £198 million. He scored on his debut but although his season ended with injury, he still scored 28 goals in 30 games and lifted the French league title. He won the title again in 2019.

HIS GAME RATED!

 Neymar is dazzling on the ball and is famous for his mega quick dribbling!

✓ *He's a super skilful finisher and he can score goals with both feet!*

 His flash play can be a bit too selfish sometimes, but he's still awesome!

PLAYER STATS

PACE
92

POWER
60

SHOOTING
86

DEFENDING
50

HEADERS
59

SKILL
96

STAT ATTACK!

105

Neymar scored 105 goals in just four seasons with Barcelona. That's red hot!

2

While playing for Brazilian club Santos, Neymar was voted South American Footballer of the Year twice. The only other Santos player to win the award was the legendary Pele.

11

He wore the number 11 shirt at Barca and Santos, but he swapped it for the number 10 when he joined PSG – the same number he wears for Brazil.

DID YOU KNOW?

The Brazilian superstar won an Olympic gold medal in 2016. He scored in the final as Brazil beat Germany on pens.

7

He has scored seven goals against PSG when playing for other teams. No wonder they wanted to sign him!

SERGIO AGUERO

Striker

Club: Manchester City	**Country:** Argentina
DOB: 02/06/1988	**International Debut:** 03/09/2006 v Brazil
Place of Birth: Buenos Aires, Argentina	**International Caps:** 97
Transfer Value: £56 million	**International Goals:** 41
Strongest Foot: Right	**Top Skill:** Expert finishing

When the mega cool Man. City goal machine started his career with Independiente in 2003, he was the youngest player in the Argentine first division – at just 15 years old, he broke a record set by Diego Maradona in 1976. But it was after joining Atletico Madrid in 2006 that he really built his rep, scoring over 100 goals in five seasons and winning the Europa League. He signed for Man. City in 2011 and celebrated his first Prem goal just nine minutes into his debut. But it was the final game of that season that made him a legend when he scored the last-minute net buster that won City their first title in 44 years. His goal celebration was bonkers and it robbed rivals Man. United of the trophy too. He's become one of the best strikers in Premier League history and not only is he now City's all-time top scorer, but he also holds the record for the most Prem hat-tricks!

HIS GAME RATED!

 He has the strength and blistering pace to beat defenders with ease!

 He favours his right foot, but he's comfortable scoring with his left too!

 Strong on the ball, he's not as good at pressing to win it back!

PLAYER STATS

PACE
88

POWER
75

SHOOTING
93

DEFENDING
50

HEADERS
79

SKILL
92

DID YOU KNOW?

Sergio Aguero was once married to the youngest daughter of footy legend Diego Maradona!

L SUAREZ

9

STAT ATTACK!

Aguero won his only Olympic gold medal when Argentina beat Nigeria in the Olympic football final in 2008.

He scored 26 goals on his way to winning the Premier League Golden Boot in the 2014-15 season. Total star!

The City top man won four Prem titles in his first eight seasons in England.

After bagging five against Newcastle in 2015, Sergio equalled the record for the most goals scored in a single Premier League game!

It took him just 147 games to score 100 Prem goals – only Harry Kane and Alan Shearer have done it quicker!

PIERRE-EMERICK
AUBAMEYANG

Forward

Club: Arsenal	**Country:** Gabon
DOB: 18/06/1989	**International Debut:** 28/03/2009 v Morocco
Place of Birth: Laval, France	**International Caps:** 63
Transfer Value: £61 million	**International Goals:** 25
Strongest Foot: Right	**Top Skill:** Pace

Auba got off the mark ultra-quickly in the Prem by scoring in his first game for Arsenal, but he had started fast at Borussia Dortmund too, bagging a hat-trick on his Bundesliga debut. His speed is his biggest asset and he was once timed running faster over 30 metres than Olympic sprinter Usain Bolt, which means his sudden bursts of pace can terrify defences. He's certainly a deadly goal scorer and he has claimed the Golden Boot in both Germany and England. Famous for his mega front flips, his wicked goal celebrations have also included pulling on superhero masks like Batman and Spiderman. In international footy, Auba had his choice of four teams. He could have played for Italy, where he lived as a kid, or France, where he was born, or Spain, because his mum is Spanish! But instead he's now the captain of Gabon – as his dad once was too. That's epic.

HIS GAME RATED!

 Auba is a penalty-box poacher – he's totally deadly in the box!

 He uses his blistering pace to make darting runs and create chances!

 His crossing isn't really the best and he's not so strong in the air!

PLAYER STATS

PACE
96

POWER
72

SHOOTING
88

DEFENDING
50

HEADERS
78

SKILL
79

STAT ATTACK!

2

When he won the Golden Boot, just two of his 22 Prem goals were with his left foot and none were headers!

DID YOU KNOW?

His dad worked for AC Milan as a scout, so Auba and his brothers all played for Milan's youth team.

Auba bagged 31 league goals for Dortmund in the 2016-17 season, which made him the Bundesliga's top scorer ahead of Robert Lewandowski!

31

17

He wears the number 14 shirt for the Gunners, but he was always number 17 at Dortmund!

22

His 22 goal tally in 2018-19 gave him a share of the Premier League Golden Boot. He was tied with Sadio Mane and Mo Salah!

MARCUS RASHFORD

Forward

Club: Manchester United	**Country:** England
DOB: 31/10/1997	**International Debut:** 27/05/2016 v Australia
Place of Birth: Wythenshawe, England	**International Caps:** 38
Transfer Value: £90 million	**International Goals:** 10
Strongest Foot: Right	**Top Skill:** Running into space

Marcus Rashford has been in red hot form for so long now that it's shocking to think that he's still only in his early 20s. Just how good can this England young gun get? He was the real breakout star of the 2015-16 season and he hasn't looked back since. He made his Man. United debut in the Europa League in February 2016 and he netted twice to become the club's youngest goal scorer in a European game. He scored two more against Arsenal just three days later on his Premier League debut. And before the end of the season, he had scored in his first England game too. Since then, he's just got better and better. He has the power, explosive speed and awesome dribbling skills to terrify opponents and when he runs at defenders at top speed, there is little they can do to stop him. He's already right on course to become an Old Trafford legend!

HIS GAME RATED!

 His quick bursts of pace make him difficult to defend against!

✓ His movement is wicked and helps him create loads of chances!

✗ 'Rash' can be a bit rash and he needs to make better decisions!

PLAYER STATS

PACE
93

POWER
78

SHOOTING
86

DEFENDING
53

HEADERS
80

SKILL
85

GOAL!

DID YOU KNOW?

When he was just five, Rash watched his first game at Old Trafford and saw Brazil star Ronaldo score a hat-trick for Real Madrid!

STAT ATTACK!

18
He was only 18 when he hit his first international goal. It made him the youngest England player to score on his debut, breaking a record that had stood since 1938!

He hasn't always been United's number 10 – he inherited the shirt after Zlatan Ibrahimovic quit Old Trafford. He started off as Man. United's number 39!

39

1
Rashford scored in his first games in the Prem, League Cup, Europa League and Champions League!

It took Rash 38 games for the famous Three Lions to score his first 10 England goals. That's good going!

38

4
He picked up four winners' medals in his first four seasons, winning the FA Cup, EFL Cup, Community Shield and Europa League!

ANTOINE GRIEZMANN

Forward

Club: Barcelona

DOB: 21/03/1991

Place of Birth: Macon, France

Transfer Value: £115 million

Strongest Foot: Left

Country: France

International Debut: 05/03/2014 v Netherlands

International Caps: 78

International Goals: 30

Top Skill: Creating space

French footy superstar Antoine Griezmann has spent his whole career in Spain. When he was a kid, French clubs thought he was too small, so at just 13 his parents let him move to Spain to chase his dream of becoming a pro footballer. He clinched his first winners' medal with Real Sociedad, and went on to make a mega name for himself with Atletico Madrid, where he won the Europa League and the UEFA Super Cup. He's been a huge star for his country too and although France lost out to Portugal in the final of Euro 2016, Griezmann was voted the tournament's best player and he finished as its top scorer. Two years later, he was a winner when he helped France lift the World Cup. Scoring in the final, he was also voted Man of the Match. Barcelona paid a jaw-dropping £107 million to sign him in 2019, making him the fourth most expensive footballer of all time.

HIS GAME RATED!

 Grizi scores mind-blowing goals and he sets them up too!

 He's got awesome skills but still works hard for the team!

 He may have top skills but dribbling isn't the best part of his game!

PLAYER STATS

PACE
83

POWER
70

SHOOTING
89

DEFENDING
55

HEADERS
82

SKILL
91

MATCH! 43

STAT ATTACK!

The French goal machine netted 133 times in 257 games in his four seasons at Atletico Madrid.

Atletico Madrid beat Marseille 3-0 in the 2018 Europa League Final thanks to a pair of goals from Griezmann. Top man!

2

Hitting six goals at the Euro 2016 finals earned Grizi the Golden Boot as the tournament's top scorer. That's epic!

6

DID YOU KNOW?
In 2017 he played the voice of Superman in the French version of 'The Lego Batman Movie'.

883

He spent an awesome 883 minutes on the pitch during France's Euro 2020 qualifying campaign, but he only scored three goals!

SON HEUNG-MIN

Forward

Club: Tottenham	**Country:** South Korea
DOB: 08/07/1992	**International Debut:** 30/12/2010 v Syria
Place of Birth: Chuncheon, South Korea	**International Caps:** 87
Transfer Value: £69 million	**International Goals:** 26
Strongest Foot: Right	**Top Skill:** Dribbling

A mega star in South Korea, Son Heung-Min has been described as the David Beckham of Asia thanks to his style of play and icon status in his home country. As a young footy star he learnt his trade in Germany, playing for Hamburg and Bayer Leverkusen, but when Spurs signed him for £22 million in 2015, it made him the most expensive Asian player in footy history. Since then he's built a rep for being one of the hottest players in the Prem.

Whether it's playing on the left wing or as a second striker for Tottenham, he's always shown off his electric pace and his deadly finishing, but he's a real team player too and he's currently the captain of South Korea. He starred for his country at two World Cups and even scored in their famous victory over Germany at Russia 2018. His hero is Cristiano Ronaldo and he's certainly lived up to his nickname of 'Sonaldo'.

HIS GAME RATED!

 He's got explosive pace and it's a struggle to catch up with him!

 Son's off-the-ball runs make him difficult to defend against!

✗ *He's not the best crosser of the ball and he prefers to drive into the box!*

PLAYER STATS

PACE
89

POWER
72

SHOOTING
88

DEFENDING
52

HEADERS
61

SKILL
89

DID YOU KNOW?

His dad was a pro footballer and he used to make Son practise keepie-uppies for hours and hours!

STAT ATTACK!

7

He wears the number 7 shirt for Spurs, just like he did for Leverkusen.

9

He has a wicked record against Dortmund. He's scored nine goals against the club – four for Hamburg, one for Bayer Leverkusen and four for Spurs.

905

Son spent 905 minutes on the pitch in Tottenham's run to the 2019 Champions League final. He played 12 out of 13 games!

42

In his first four seasons at Spurs, Son scored 42 Prem goals – 23 with his right foot, 17 with his left and two with his head!

3

He's played at two World Cups and has scored three goals, including one of the best strikes of the 2018 World Cup against Mexico.

KYLIAN MBAPPE

Forward

Club: Paris Saint-Germain

DOB: 20/12/1998

Place of Birth: Paris, France

Transfer Value: £180 million

Strongest Foot: Right

Country: France

International Debut: 25/03/2017 v Luxembourg

International Caps: 34

International Goals: 13

Top Skill: Stepovers

Kylian Mbappe is one of the best young players in the world at the moment, but he's only going to get better and better. He has the kind of blistering pace that defenders struggle to match and he has wicked dribbling skills too. He is always cool under pressure and pretty deadly in front of goal. He began his career at Monaco, where he won his first French league title, and he racked up another two after his £165.7 million transfer to Paris Saint-Germain, which made him the most expensive teenager on the planet. He's not just a hero for his club, he's become a mega star for his country too. He lit up the 2018 World Cup with his crazy skills and he was voted the best young player at the tournament. Better still, he picked up a winners' medal and scored a goal that helped France beat Croatia, making him the first teen since Pele to score in a World Cup final. He really is the biz!

HIS GAME RATED!

 He's got incredibly quick feet and knows how to use them!

✓ *His powerful running can destroy defenders and wreck opponents!*

 He's not a defender but he really needs to improve his tackling!

x

PLAYER STATS

PACE
98

POWER
85

SHOOTING
86

DEFENDING
50

HEADERS
75

SKILL
92

STAT ATTACK!

He's PSG's lucky number 7 now, but when he first moved to Paris he wore the 29 shirt.

29

12

He's a wicked dribbler - in 534 minutes on the pitch at the 2018 World Cup, he ran 12 miles with the ball at his feet.

DID YOU KNOW?

When he was 11, Mbappe played a trial game for Chelsea against Charlton Athletic!

33

In 2018-19 he scored 33 goals in 29 games for PSG. That made him the French league's top scorer.

100

The France young gun hit the 100th pro goal of his career away to Andorra in 2019.

JOAO FELIX

Forward

Club: Atletico Madrid	**Country:** Portugal
DOB: 10/11/1999	**International Debut:** 05/06/2019 v Switzerland
Place of Birth: Viseu, Portugal	**International Caps:** 4
Transfer Value: £95 million	**International Goals:** 0
Strongest Foot: Right	**Top Skill:** First touch

The newest hot shot on the block, in just one season in the Benfica first-team Joao Felix caused shockwaves with his skilful close control and his flash style of play. He scored in the Lisbon derby against Sporting in his second game for Benfica, but it was a hat-trick in the Europa League quarter-final win over Frankfurt that caught the attention of teams across Europe. Man. United and Liverpool were among the clubs sniffing around but it was Atletico Madrid that stumped up the £113 million needed to clinch his signature. That hefty transfer fee made him the third most expensive star in footy history. It also made him the second most expensive teenager, after Kylian Mbappe, so he's in pretty awesome company. He wrapped up his time at Benfica by winning the Portuguese league title and he has looked good with his dazzling early form in Madrid.

HIS GAME RATED!

✓ His dribbling skills get him out of trouble when space is tight!

✓ He has footy vision and his eye for a quality pass is first class!

✗ He's a bit lightweight and can be out-muscled by stronger opponents!

PACE
80

POWER
73

SHOOTING
81

DEFENDING
51

HEADERS
67

SKILL
83

PLAYER STATS

DID YOU KNOW?

Porto let Felix go as a 15-year-old because he was too small!

STAT ATTACK!

10

He won 10 caps for Portugal's Under-21 side and scored four goals. He also played for the U18s and the U19s!

Felix scored three goals in Benfica's 4-2 defeat of Frankfurt. At 19 years and 152 days old, that made him the youngest player to score a Europa League hat-trick. Wicked!

3

15

In his one season with Benfica, the teenage hot shot bagged 15 league goals in 26 games and won the Portuguese league title. Get in!

On joining Atletico, he was given the number 7 shirt, previously worn by Antoine Griezmann!

7

70

He debuted for Portugal in the Nations League semi against Switzerland, playing the first 70 minutes of the match.

FIRST XI!

Can you answer these 11 tough footy questions?

1. How many times has Neymar been voted South American Footballer of the Year - once, twice or three times?

2. Only two players have scored 100 Premier League goals quicker than Man. City striker Sergio Aguero. Can you name them?

3. Name the team Man. United's Marcus Rashford scored against on his Premier League debut!

4. Which club did Lionel Messi score his first Barcelona hat-trick against?

5. How many times has Cristiano Ronaldo won the Champo League?

6. Can you name the team that Harry Kane scored a hat-trick against at the 2018 FIFA World Cup?

7. How many goals did Antoine Griezmann score at Euro 2016 to win the Golden Boot?

8. Which French football club gave Kylian Mbappe his professional debut – Monaco or Paris Saint-Germain?

9. Which country does Spurs forward Son Heung-Min play for?

10. Robert Lewandowski set a Champions League record in 2019 by scoring four goals in under 15 minutes. Can you name the team he was playing against?

11. Pierre-Emerick Aubameyang joined Arsenal from which German team – Bayern Munich or Dortmund?

What Nationality?

Match the stars with the country they play for!

1
Pierre-E Aubameyang

2
Joao Felix

3
Robert Lewandowski

4
Sergio Aguero

Poland

A

Argentina

B

Gabon

C

Portugal

D

1 & C

 MATCH!

ANAGRAMS!

Rearrange the letters to find five top super strikers.

1. SCRUMA SHARDROF

2. INETONA NAGZMIREN

3. NIOELL SEMIS

4. YAHRR KEAN

5. YANILK PEMPAB

QUIZ ANSWERS!

FIRST XI

1. Twice
2. Harry Kane & Alan Shearer
3. Arsenal
4. Real Madrid
5. Five
6. Panama
7. Six
8. Monaco
9. South Korea
10. Red Star Belgrade
11. Borussia Dortmund

WHAT NATIONALITY?

1. C
2. D
3. A
4. B

ANAGRAMS

1. Marcus Rashford
2. Antoine Griezmann
3. Lionel Messi
4. Harry Kane
5. Kylian Mbappe

MIDFIELDERS & WINGERS

KEVIN
DE BRUYNE

Midfielder

Club: Manchester City	**Country:** Belgium
DOB: 28/06/1991	**International Debut:** 11/08/2010 v Finland
Place of Birth: Drongen, Belgium	**International Caps:** 74
Transfer Value: £120 million	**International Goals:** 19
Strongest Foot: Right	**Top Skill:** Footy intelligence

Cool on the ball, Kevin De Bruyne really is a super chilled footy superstar. In his time at Man. City, he has established himself as one of Europe's most awesome and consistent midfielders. But after failing to make the grade at Chelsea under Jose Mourinho early in his career, it all could have been so different. A transfer out of Stamford Bridge allowed the Belgian playmaker to reinvent himself at Wolfsburg and it wasn't very long before he was voted Germany's Footballer of the Year. Man. City soon came calling and paid a cool £55 million to bring him to the Etihad Stadium, where he has since won two Premier League titles. He was also the star of the 2019 FA Cup Final, scoring the third goal in City's 6-0 demolition of Watford and picking up the Man of the Match award, despite only coming on the pitch as a second-half substitute. Top man!

HIS GAME RATED!

✓ *He's a clever playmaker and he can spot passes that others can't see!*

✓ *His positioning is top notch and he loves to shoot from distance!*

✗ *Improving his tackling would make him the perfect midfielder!*

PLAYER STATS

PACE
80

POWER
80

SHOOTING
89

DEFENDING
66

HEADERS
53

SKILL
92

STAT ATTACK!

DID YOU KNOW?

De Bruyne could have played for the small African nation of Burundi, as his mother was born there!

De Bruyne played only three Prem games in his two years at Chelsea. He spent most of his time out on loan.

He made seven assists as Belgium qualified for the finals of Euro 2020 – the joint second highest tally in qualification.

He was voted Man. City's Player of the Season twice in his first four seasons at the club. What a star!

De Bruyne may have become a big hit at Man. City, but he played just nine games for Chelsea – and only three of those were in the Premier League!

SADIO MANE

Winger

Club: Liverpool

DOB: 10/04/1992

Place of Birth: Sedhiou, Senegal

Transfer Value: £140 million

Strongest Foot: Right

Country: Senegal

International Debut: 25/05/2012 v Morocco

International Caps: 69

International Goals: 19

Top Skill: Darting runs

Along with Mohamed Salah and Roberto Firmino, Mane is one of the stars of Liverpool's explosive front line, which has been destroying defences around Europe for the past few seasons. A right-footed winger who has mostly been used on the left at Liverpool, he has pace to burn. His movement is awesome on the ball and he's a real threat off it, as he loves to make darting runs into the box to create the space to score. After spells in France with Metz, in Austria with Salzburg and in the Premier League with Southampton, he really came into his own after joining Liverpool in 2016 and by the end of his first season he was voted the club's Player of the Year. He scored Liverpool's only goal in the 2018 Champions League Final when the Reds lost to Real Madrid, but he picked up a winners' medal a year later. And since then, he just keeps getting better!

HIS GAME RATED!

✓ *Comfortable on either wing or up front, he's the perfect attacker!*

✓ *His movement is quick, clever and difficult for defenders to track!*

✗ *His first touch has been known to let him down from time to time!*

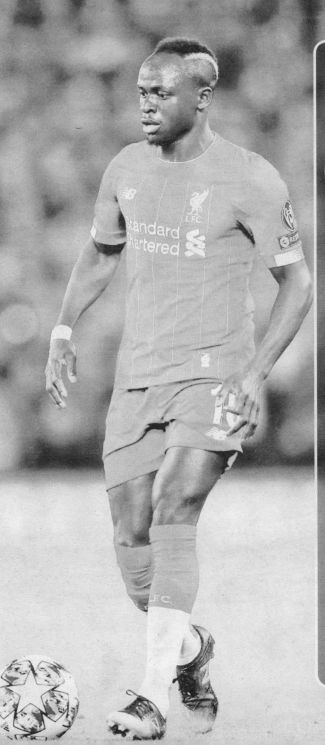

PLAYER STATS

PACE
96

POWER
77

SHOOTING
86

DEFENDING
53

HEADERS
79

SKILL
91

DID YOU KNOW?

Mane helped Senegal to a draw with Great Britain at Old Trafford during the 2012 Olympics!

STAT ATTACK!

4

He netted four against Liverpool in one season while playing for Southampton. The Reds signed him just a few months later.

He scored 10 Champions League goals in 2017-18. Salah and Firmino also scored 10, making the three team-mates joint second highest scorers in the comp. Weird but true!

10

176

He holds the record for the quickest Prem hat-trick ever, netting three times for Southampton against Aston Villa in 176 seconds in 2015. Just wow!

Mane scored twice in the 2019 UEFA Super Cup as Liverpool beat Chelsea on pens to lift the trophy.

2

22

He bagged 22 goals in 2018-19, earning him a share of the Prem Golden Boot – he was tied with Aubameyang and Salah.

FRENKIE DE JONG

Midfielder

Club: Barcelona	**Country:** Netherlands
DOB: 12/05/1997	**International Debut:** 06/09/2018 v Peru
Place of Birth: Gorinchem, Netherlands	**International Caps:** 15
Transfer Value: £74 million	**International Goals:** 1
Strongest Foot: Right	**Top Skill:** Pinpoint passing

The wicked Dutch midfielder was one of Europe's most sought-after young players, with Man. City and PSG among the chasing pack. But it was Barcelona that stumped up a whopping £65 million to sign him from Ajax in 2019. Tipped to be a future legend of the game, he can play almost anywhere on the pitch but he seems most suited to a defensive midfield role where he is able to dictate the play. He's totally unflappable on the ball and even when pressed or surrounded by opponents, he can usually find a way to play out to a team-mate and launch an attack from nothing. Before leaving for Barcelona, he helped Ajax to win the club's first league and cup double for 17 years and he was voted the Dutch top flight's Player of the Season. But he'll be hoping there will be many more medals and trophies ahead of him now that he's with one of the world's biggest clubs.

HIS GAME RATED!

 He's fantastic at keeping hold of the ball under pressure!

 His work-rate is second to none and he has great technique!

✗ *His finishing needs to develop a little to make him the best!*

PACE
80

POWER
78

SHOOTING
70

DEFENDING
79

HEADERS
70

SKILL
90

STAT ATTACK!

1

Willem II sold De Jong to Ajax for £1 three years before his £65 million transfer to Barca. But thankfully they asked for a percentage of any future sale. Phew!

21

He wears the number 21 on his shirt as a tribute to his grandad, who was born on April 21st.

DID YOU KNOW?
De Jong swapped shirts with Kylian Mbappe when the Netherlands played France in 2018!

82

He played for Ajax in the 2017 Europa League Final, coming on as a sub in the 82nd minute. He collected a runners-up medal after losing to Man. United.

31

He played in 31 of Ajax's 34 league games as they won the Dutch title in 2018-19. He scored four goals too.

EDEN
HAZARD

Left winger

Club: Real Madrid

DOB: 07/01/1991

Place of Birth: La Louviere, Belgium

Transfer Value: £135 million

Strongest Foot: Right

Country: Belgium

International Debut: 19/11/2008 v Luxembourg

International Caps: 106

International Goals: 32

Top Skill: Dribbling

In seven seasons at Chelsea, Eden Hazard proved to be one of the best players that the Premier League has ever seen. He wowed fans with his skilful dribbling and his flash tricks. He also won a bucket load of medals, including two Prem titles to go with his French Ligue 1 title won at Lille. He was awarded the Silver Ball too, after helping Belgium to third place in the 2018 World Cup. A big game player, he always delivers when it matters and his vital goals include the winner in the 2018 FA Cup Final and another two strikes in the 2019 Europa League Final. That night, he was not only voted the Man of the Match but the Europa League's Player of the Season. It seems that Real Madrid have signed a player at the top of his game - now he just needs to light up La Liga in the same way as he dazzled the Prem. But that should be no problem for the Haz man!

HIS GAME RATED!

 His low centre of gravity means he can skip past defences with ease!

 He's the wizard of dribble and it's hard to stop his mazy runs!

 His defending is the only real weakness in his game!

PLAYER STATS

PACE
90

POWER
65

SHOOTING
86

DEFENDING
50

HEADERS
59

SKILL
95

MATCH! 77

DID YOU KNOW?

His brothers are footballers and one even played alongside him at the 2018 World Cup!

STAT ATTACK!

15

In his final season at Chelsea he topped the Premier League assists chart, setting up 15 goals! Coolio!

During the 2018 World Cup, he dribbled into the opposition penalty area 19 times.

19

4

Voted Chelsea's Player of the Year four times in seven seasons, he was also voted the club's Players' Player of the Year twice. What a hero!

He racked up 85 goals and 54 assists in 245 Prem games for Chelsea.

85

11,635

Hazard made an amazing 11,635 passes in his seven seasons in the Prem!

N'GOLO
KANTE

Defensive midfielder

Club: Chelsea	**Country:** France
DOB: 29/03/1991	**International Debut:** 25/03/2016 v Netherlands
Place of Birth: Paris, France	**International Caps:** 39
Transfer Value: £70 million	**International Goals:** 1
Strongest Foot: Right	**Top Skill:** Super stamina

There are few central midfielders in world footy who can both attack and defend with the same quality as N'Golo Kante. An outrageously good player, he has won nearly everything there is to win in the game, including the Prem with both Leicester City and Chelsea, the FA Cup and the Europa League with Chelsea, and the World Cup with France. More than that, he's been voted Player of the Year in both England and France, so he's a real hero everywhere. Through his natural footballing intelligence and his sheer hard work, he has managed to turn himself into the complete midfielder. In fact, footy fans across Europe love his simple, no-nonsense playing style. He doesn't score too many goals, but when he's on top form he's a real destroyer and he knows exactly how to break up attacks and when to drive forward to launch counter-attacks. He really is the business!

HIS GAME RATED!

 A really hard-working ball winner, he can put a stop to any attack!

 He reads the game well and has great positional awareness!

 His lack of height means that he's not that great in the air!

PLAYER STATS

PACE
81

POWER
86

SHOOTING
70

DEFENDING
90

HEADERS
57

SKILL
81

STAT ATTACK!

Kante is one of only 10 players to win the Premier League with two different clubs - but the only one to have done it in consecutive years!

175

When Leicester won the Prem in 2015-16, he made 175 tackles. This was more than any other player.

54

In his first five seasons in the Prem, Kante has averaged 54 passes a game!

156

He made 156 interceptions the year Leicester won the Prem, more than any other player!

SERGE GNABRY

Winger

Club: Bayern Munich

DOB: 14/07/1995

Place of Birth: Stuttgart, Germany

Transfer Value: £80 million

Strongest Foot: Right

Country: Germany

International Debut: 11/11/2016 v San Marino

International Caps: 13

International Goals: 13

Top Skill: One-on-ones

Serge Gnabry could be Germany's next footy mega star but it won't make Arsenal fans very happy. He was a former youth player at the Emirates and at just 21 he was allowed to leave the Gunners for a measly £4 million in 2015, having spent much of the previous season twiddling his thumbs on loan at West Brom. He has since reinvented himself at Bayern Munich and the 13 goals he scored in his first season helped win the German league and cup double. He was even voted Bayern's Player of the Year. He's made a similar impact on the national team, bagging a hat-trick against San Marino on his debut in 2016. He scored another hat-trick against Northern Ireland in 2019, taking his international record to 13 goals in 13 games, something only the legendary Gerd Muller has achieved for Germany before. Gnabry is becoming one of Europe's most feared attackers.

HIS GAME RATED!

 He's pretty much unstoppable in one-on-one situations!

 He's deadly when he cuts inside and shoots with power!

 His direct play can sometimes make him selfish in front of goal!

PLAYER STATS

PACE
93

POWER
76

SHOOTING
85

DEFENDING
50

HEADERS
50

SKILL
90

MATCH! 85

DID YOU KNOW?

He was a talented sprinter growing up but he chose footy over athletics!

STAT ATTACK!

6

He was joint top scorer at the 2016 Olympics with six goals, but Germany lost the gold medal to Brazil on pens!

He joined Arsenal at 16 and went on to play 10 Prem games for the club before leaving for the Bundesliga!

4,000

He scored Bayern Munich's 4,000th Bundesliga goal in a game against Borussia Monchengladbach in 2019!

It took him 11 games to bag 10 international goals, making him the quickest player to do this for Germany. He beat Miroslav Klose's record by two games.

4

The former Gunner scored four goals as Bayern thrashed Spurs 7-2 away in the Champions League. What a mega star!

HAKIM ZIYECH

Attacking midfielder

Club: Chelsea	**Country:** Morocco
DOB: 19/03/1993	**International Debut:** 09/10/2015 v Ivory Coast
Place of Birth: Dronten, Netherlands	**International Caps:** 32
Transfer Value: £41 million	**International Goals:** 14
Strongest Foot: Left	**Top Skill:** Creating chances

Hakim Ziyech had been in pretty spectacular form for Ajax in recent seasons. A versatile midfielder who has shown he can perform in all kinds of roles for his team, he is not only a solid goal scorer himself but he's a wicked creator of scoring chances for his team-mates too. In fact, he had topped the Dutch assists chart four times in just five seasons and he was voted the country's Footballer of the Year in 2018. The following season he helped Ajax to the highs of a Dutch league and cup double, but he also experienced the gut-wrenching lows of defeat in the Champions League semi-finals to Spurs. He has continued to work on his style and has improved as a player. As a result, his performances attracted the attention of Chelsea, who agreed for him to join the club in the summer of 2020 for a fee of £36.6 million. He could become the next huge star of the game!

HIS GAME RATED!

 He's well known for his pinpoint long-range passing!

 Great with the ball, he has loads of pace and wicked skills!

 Sometimes he needs to keep his play a little more simple!

PLAYER STATS

PACE
80

POWER
71

SHOOTING
77

DEFENDING
55

HEADERS
59

SKILL
87

STAT ATTACK!

4

The best creator in the Netherlands, he has topped the Dutch assists chart four times in five years. That's awesome!

DID YOU KNOW?

He won caps for the Netherlands at youth level before choosing to play for Morocco!

3

By 2019 he had made the Dutch league's Team of the Year three times. He also made the 2018-19 Champions League Squad of the Season!

13

When Ajax won the league in 2019, he set-up 13 goals in 29 games. He also scored 16 himself. Get in there!

265

He spent 265 minutes on the pitch during Morocco's three games at the 2018 World Cup.

PAUL POGBA

Midfielder

Club: Manchester United	**Country:** France
DOB: 15/03/1993	**International Debut:** 22/03/2013 v Georgia
Place of Birth: Lagny-sur-Marne, France	**International Caps:** 69
Transfer Value: £85 million	**International Goals:** 10
Strongest Foot: Right	**Top Skill:** Through balls

Love him or hate him, every footy fan has an opinion on Paul Pogba. He's that crazy good midfielder with a taste for mad haircuts and a tendency to sulk. He first joined Man. United at just 16, but with his pitch time limited he jumped ship to Juventus in 2012, having played just three Prem games. At Juventus, Pog was given the freedom to express himself and his creative midfield play helped the club to grab four Italian league titles in as many years, plus two Italian Cups. But even this wasn't enough to keep Pogba happy and he returned to Old Trafford in 2016, with United breaking the British transfer record to sign him again. A big deal in his home country, he was one of the stars of the French team that finished as runners up at Euro 2016. Two years later he went one better, lifting the World Cup trophy after scoring in the final. It doesn't get any better than that!

HIS GAME RATED!

 His midfield creativity can help break down the strongest of defences!

 He can see passes that other players can only dream of!

 He sometimes gets criticised by pundits for his work-rate!

PLAYER STATS

PACE
77

POWER
87

SHOOTING
84

DEFENDING
67

HEADERS
70

SKILL
88

MATCH! 93

DID YOU KNOW?
He has two older brothers who are both pro footballers!

STAT ATTACK!

Between his two stints at Man. United he played 178 games for Juventus and scored 34 goals!

When he first broke into the Man. United team he wore 42 on his back. When he returned to Old Trafford, he made the number 6 shirt his own!

He won four Serie A league titles in his four seasons with Juve!

Pogba hit a top speed of 18 miles an hour during the 2018 World Cup Final. He's a boy racer!

In his first 100 Prem games for Man. United, he scored 24 goals. That's almost one every four games!

MOHAMED SALAH

Right winger

Club: Liverpool	**Country:** Egypt
DOB: 15/06/1992	**International Debut:** 03/09/2011 v Sierra Leone
Place of Birth: Nagrig, Egypt	**International Caps:** 67
Transfer Value: £145 million	**International Goals:** 41
Strongest Foot: Left	**Top Skill:** Finishing

Whatever he goes on to do in footy, Mo Salah will always be remembered for his incredible debut season at Liverpool. That year he broke the Prem scoring record, bagging 32 goals in just 36 games. Not bad for a winger! He'd failed to impress in Chelsea colours early in his career and spent much of his time out on loan, but he attracted the attention of Liverpool after reigniting his career at Roma. Since then, he's gone on to achieve mega stardom at Anfield. His goals helped power the club to two Champions League finals in a row, but his injury early in the 2018 final spoilt Liverpool's chances of success. A year later he finally picked up a winners' medal, netting a pen as the Reds lifted the trophy. Nicknamed the Egyptian Messi, he's a superstar in his home country too and he's won the African Footballer of the Year award twice. He's fast becoming a living legend!

HIS GAME RATED!

 He loves to cut in from the right wing and shoot with his left foot!

 No-one can stop him when he's running with the ball at his feet!

 He's so focused on scoring himself that he can be a bit selfish!

PLAYER STATS

PACE
94

POWER
78

SHOOTING
88

DEFENDING
53

HEADERS
62

SKILL
91

MATCH! 97

STAT ATTACK!

He's been a goal machine for the Reds but he wasn't a hit for the Blues. He scored just twice for Chelsea in two years with the club!

2

32

In the 2017-18 season, Mo outscored three Prem clubs. His 32-goal tally was more than the number of goals scored by West Brom, Swansea and Huddersfield!

DID YOU KNOW?

He's famous as a number 11 at Liverpool, but when Mo played in Italy for Fiorentina, he wore the less famous number 74 shirt!

3

Mo was the first player ever to win the Prem's Player of the Month award three times in the same season!

72

It took Mo just 72 games to score 50 Prem goals. Only Andy Cole (65 games), Alan Shearer (66) and Ruud van Nistelrooy (68) have hit this target quicker!

RAHEEM STERLING

Winger

Club: Manchester City

DOB: 08/12/1994

Place of Birth: Kingston, Jamaica

Transfer Value: £115 million

Strongest Foot: Right

Country: England

International Debut: 14/11/2012 v Sweden

International Caps: 56

International Goals: 12

Top Skill: Electric speed

Raheem was born in Jamaica but he moved to England with his mum when he was just five. When he was growing up in West London, he could see the famous Wembley arch from his home in Harlesden and now, thanks to his wicked footy skills, he's become one of the best players to have scored on that legendary Wembley pitch. He first made a name for himself at Liverpool, but a transfer to Man. City made him the most expensive English player in history and he has flourished under Pep Guardiola's coaching. Always one of the flashiest players in the Prem, his game has improved each season. Where fans once booed him for his diving antics, now he's cheered as one of England's true world-class talents. And at Man. City the rewards have come – he's won two Prem titles, three EFL Cups and the FA Cup, scoring twice in the final in 2019. He's a major star!

HIS GAME RATED!

✓ He's capable of burning opponents with his speed and acceleration!

✓ His quick movement and fancy footwork can bamboozle defenders!

✗ Sometimes his shooting technique can be a little hit or miss!

PACE
94

POWER
60

SHOOTING
83

DEFENDING
52

HEADERS
50

SKILL
93

DID YOU KNOW?

When he was 16, Liverpool only included him in the senior squad for the first time because he was off school for his half-term hols!

STAT ATTACK!

Before signing for Man. City, he played 129 games in all comps for Liverpool, scoring 23 goals!

Up to the end of the 2018-19 season, he had hit the woodwork 16 times in his Premier League career!

18

When Man. City won the Prem in 2017-18, he scored 18 goals in 33 games. That's the most he's scored in a league season. He also set up 11 goals for his team mates!

He's scored one hat-trick for England – that was against the Czech Republic at Wembley in 2019!

8

Sterling was England's second highest scorer during the Euro 2020 qualifiers, bagging eight goals. Only Harry Kane scored more for the Three Lions!

JADON
SANCHO

Winger

Club: Borussia Dortmund	**Country:** England
DOB: 25/03/2000	**International Debut:** 12/10/2018 v Croatia
Place of Birth: Camberwell, England	**International Caps:** 11
Transfer Value: £100 million	**International Goals:** 2
Strongest Foot: Right	**Top Skill:** Decision making

One of the most electrifying young players in the game today, Jadon Sancho is the brightest talent to have come out of the Man. City academy in recent years, but he chose to take a different route to success. Worried that he stood little chance of breaking into City's star-studded first team, he signed for top German club Borussia Dortmund and smashed it in the Bundesliga instead. After showing what he could do for Dortmund,

Sancho earned his first cap against Croatia in 2018 – this made him the second youngest player to make his England debut in a competitive match. After a stunning second season with Dortmund, he won his first trophy with the club in 2019, scoring in a 2-0 victory over Bayern Munich in the German Super Cup. Barely out of his teens, he just keeps improving – no wonder he is being linked with a move to some of the biggest clubs in footy!

HIS GAME RATED!

 His through balls and cut backs are absolutely top notch!

 He always makes the right pass at just the right time!

 His left foot is decent but it isn't in the same class as his right!

PLAYER STATS

PACE
90

POWER
71

SHOOTING
82

DEFENDING
51

HEADERS
50

SKILL
91

STAT ATTACK!

7

Sancho inherited the Dortmund number 7 shirt from Ousmane Dembele, who left the club to join Barcelona!

14

Jadon is the king of assists. He set up 14 league goals for Dortmund in the 2018-19 season. That was more assists than anyone else in the Bundesliga!

3

He racked up three goals and two assists as England won the Under-17 World Cup in 2017. These all came in the group games – Dortmund wouldn't let him play in the knockout rounds!

DID YOU KNOW?

Jadon started off with Watford, but when he was just 14 he took the brave step of moving north to join Man. City's academy!

15

He became the youngest player to score 15 Bundesliga goals when he notched against Cologne in August 2019!

FIRST XI!

Can you answer these 11 tough footy questions?

1. How many goals did Liverpool's Mo Salah score to win the Premier League Golden Boot in the 2017-18 season?

2. In which country was Man. City star Raheem Sterling born?

3. N'Golo Kante has won the Premier League with two clubs. Can you name them?

4. Name the Italian club Paul Pogba played for between his two stints at Man. United.

5. How many times was Eden Hazard voted Chelsea's Player of the Year – three times or four?

6. Which country did Kevin De Bruyne make his international debut against – Finland or Greece?

7. Serge Gnabry has played in the Premier League for two clubs. Can you name both of them?

8. Who wore the number seven shirt at Dortmund before it was given to Jadon Sancho?

9. Which Dutch club did Frenkie De Jong play for before joining Barcelona?

10. Which year did Sadio Mane score for Liverpool in the Champions League final?

11. Name the country that Chelsea new boy Hakim Ziyech plays international football for.

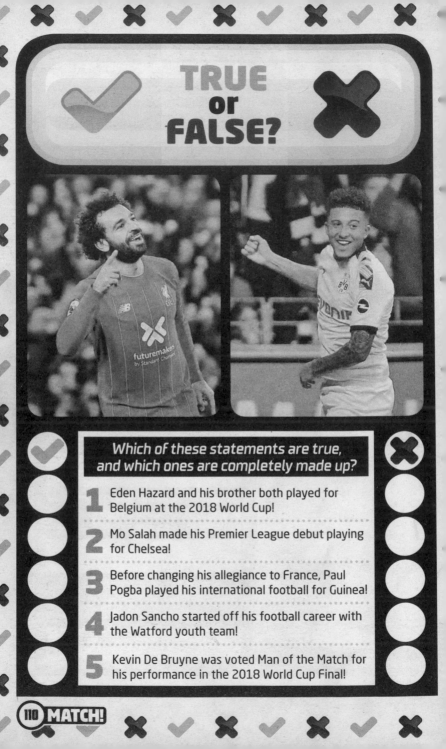

TRUE or FALSE?

Which of these statements are true, and which ones are completely made up?

1 Eden Hazard and his brother both played for Belgium at the 2018 World Cup!

2 Mo Salah made his Premier League debut playing for Chelsea!

3 Before changing his allegiance to France, Paul Pogba played his international football for Guinea!

4 Jadon Sancho started off his football career with the Watford youth team!

5 Kevin De Bruyne was voted Man of the Match for his performance in the 2018 World Cup Final!

WHO STARTED WHERE?

Match the stars to the clubs they made their pro debut with!

RAHEEM STERLING

1

EDEN HAZARD

2

N'GOLO KANTE

3

PAUL POGBA

4

A

MAN. UNITED

B

U.S. Boulogne
Côte d'Opale

BOULOGNE

C

LIVERPOOL
FOOTBALL CLUB

LIVERPOOL

D

LOSC

LILLE

1 & C

WORDSEARCH

Can you find the 20 top midfielders and wingers?

- ✓ Bale
- ✓ De Bruyne
- ✓ De Jong
- ✓ Dembele
- ✓ Di Maria
- Eriksen
- ✓ Gnabry
- Hazard
- ✓ Isco
- Jorginho

- Kante
- Mahrez
- Mane
- ✓ Pogba
- Reus
- Salah
- Sancho
- Sane
- Sterling
- Ziyech

DEFENDERS
& KEEPERS

VIRGIL VAN DIJK

Centre-back

Club: Liverpool

DOB: 08/07/1991

Place of Birth: Breda, Netherlands

Transfer Value: £100 million

Strongest Foot: Right

Country: Netherlands

International Debut: 10/10/2015 v Kazakhstan

International Caps: 33

International Goals: 4

Top Skill: Intercepting the ball

Since arriving at Anfield in 2018, Virgil van Dijk has become one of the most talked about players on the planet. Liverpool splashed out £75 million to sign him from Southampton, a world record for a defender, but it was money well spent. Since then, he's been a powerhouse at the heart of the Liverpool defence and, aside from his wicked skills as a stopper, he has also provided the Reds with some much needed leadership on the pitch. He managed to win over the fans in his very first game for the club, scoring the goal that knocked local rivals Everton out of the FA Cup - it was a towering header in front of the famous Kop too. His biggest successes are probably still ahead of him as he just keeps getting better and better, but he has already lifted the Champions League after putting in a Man of the Match display against Spurs in the 2019 final!

HIS GAME RATED!

 Cool on the ball, he's big and bold enough to deal with any striker!

 He's a very clever defender and he reads the game perfectly!

 He may be a defender but tackling isn't a big part of his game!

PACE
81

POWER
90

SHOOTING
64

DEFENDING
95

HEADERS
92

SKILL
76

DID YOU KNOW?

Virgil was voted
Premier League
Player of the
Season in 2019!

STAT ATTACK!

2

He lifted the Scottish Premiership twice in a row in the famous hooped shirt of Celtic!

He scored seven goals during his time at Southampton. He didn't score against Liverpool but he did bag one against Italian giants Inter Milan!

3,385

He spent 3,385 minutes on the pitch for the Reds during the 2018-19 Premier League season.

He's proud to wear the number 4 shirt for Liverpool but he was number 17 at Southampton and number 5 at Celtic!

The Dutch master made his Netherlands debut at the age of 24 and he is now captain of the national side!

SERGIO RAMOS

Centre-back

Club: Real Madrid	**Country:** Spain
DOB: 30/03/1986	**International Debut:** 26/03/2005 v China
Place of Birth: Camas, Spain	**International Caps:** 170
Transfer Value: £25 million	**International Goals:** 21
Strongest Foot: Right	**Top Skill:** Powerful headers

Sergio Ramos has enjoyed an awesome footy career and he's won pretty much everything there is to win in the game, including the World Cup and two European Championship titles with Spain and four Champions League titles with Real Madrid. He's quick, powerful and aggressive, always comfortable with the ball at his feet and fantastic in the air. In fact, he's one of the best defenders in football, but it's possible that he'll be better remembered for his incredible late goals, like the 93rd-minute header that took the 2014 Champions League Final to extra-time and allowed Real to snatch the trophy from local rivals Atletico. A born leader, he captains both his club and country. When he made his international debut in 2005, he became the youngest person to play for Spain for 55 years but these days, he's his country's most capped player. That's sick!

HIS GAME RATED!

✓ He's known as a centre-back but he's a pretty good right back too!

✓ He's great in the air and really knows how to score with his head!

✗ He's hot-headed and gets far too many yellow and red cards!

PLAYER STATS

PACE
71

POWER
90

SHOOTING
73

DEFENDING
91

HEADERS
93

SKILL
75

STAT ATTACK!

Sergio Ramos has been red carded 26 times while playing for Real Madrid!

26

16

In October 2019 he became only the second player after Lionel Messi to score goals in 16 La Liga seasons in a row!

Up until the end of the 2018-19 season, he had scored 84 goals for Real Madrid in all comps. Not bad for a defender!

84

4

He has lifted the Champions League trophy four times with Real Madrid – three times as captain!

DID YOU KNOW?

He was originally a striker when he signed for his first club, Sevilla!

MARC-ANDRE
TER STEGEN

Goalkeeper

Club: Barcelona	**Country:** Germany
DOB: 30/04/1992	**International Debut:** 26/05/2012 v Switzerland
Place of Birth: Monchengladbach, Germany	**International Caps:** 24
Transfer Value: £75 million	**International Goals:** 0
Strongest Foot: Right	**Top Skill:** Distribution

It took two seasons for Ter Stegen to establish himself as Barcelona's undisputed number one, but since then his wicked shot-stopping has helped him lay claim to the title of the best goalkeeper in the world. He's already won loads, including the Champions League in 2015. That year he also won UEFA's Save of the Season award for his awesome goal line save from Lewandowski in a Champions League semi against Bayern Munich. In international football he's been less lucky. His chances have been limited by the Germany gaffer's decision to stick with Manuel Neuer in goal. Ter Stegen has only been given a decent run between the posts at the 2017 Confederations Cup, where he picked up a winners' medal and was voted Man of the Match in the final. But he's a bonkers good keeper and he's still in his 20s, so time is on his side.

HIS GAME RATED!

 He's great with his hands and is a wickedly good shot-stopper!

 He reads the game well and is quick off his line to make saves!

 His international game time has been limited by rival Manuel Neuer!

REFLEXES
92

SHOT-STOP
91

AGILITY
89

CATCHING
87

KICKING
88

PEN. SAVES
90

DID YOU KNOW?
He's been called 'Messi with gloves' but he doesn't like the nickname!

STAT ATTACK!

108

He played 108 league games for Monchengladbach and kept 36 clean sheets!

In his first season with Barca, he made no league appearances. Ter Stegen was used as keeper in the Copa del Rey and the Champions League instead!

0

46

Up until the end of the 2018-19 season, he had conceded just 46 goals in 52 Champions League games!

When Barca won the league title in 2017-18, he played 37 of the team's 38 games and kept 19 clean sheets – his highest total in a league season!

19

142

In his final league season at Monchengladbach he made 142 saves and conceded just 43 goals in 34 games!

ANDY ROBERTSON

Left-back

Club: Liverpool

DOB: 11/03/1994

Place of Birth: Glasgow, Scotland

Transfer Value: £65 million

Strongest Foot: Left

Country: Scotland

International Debut: 05/03/2014 v Poland

International Caps: 34

International Goals: 3

Top Skill: Pace

Andy Robertson has not only been one of the most outstanding players in the recent Liverpool revival, he has shown himself to be the sickest left-back in Europe at the moment. An £8 million bargain bought from Hull City in 2017, he could be one of the club's greatest ever signings. And with his storming overlapping runs up the left wing, he's become an essential part of Liverpool's attacking style of play. It's no wonder they call him the Flying Scotsman. Not bad for a player who started his career as a semi-pro for Queens Park in the Scottish Third Division. In his short time at Anfield, he's managed to win the Champions League and he briefly held the Prem record for the highest number of assists made in a season by a defender until it was bettered by team-mate Trent Alexander-Arnold. Still in his mid 20s, he can surely go on to become a legend for both club and country.

HIS GAME RATED!

 He gets up the pitch and nabs more than his fair share of assists!

 He's quick to get back and defend if an attack breaks down!

 For a forward-thinking defender he doesn't score many goals!

PLAYER STATS

PACE
90

POWER
81

SHOOTING
63

DEFENDING
86

HEADERS
63

SKILL
84

MATCH! 129

STAT ATTACK!

In three seasons with Hull City, he played 99 league games – 57 were in the Premier League and 42 were in the Championship!

99

12

In Liverpool's run to Champions League glory in 2018-19, he played 12 of the team's 13 games, spending 1,008 minutes on the pitch!

His shirt number at Liverpool is 26, but he also wore this number for two of his three seasons at Hull and at Dundee United!

26

DID YOU KNOW?

He was a youth player for Celtic but the Bhoys let him go at 15!

11

He assisted his team-mates in scoring 11 goals in the 2018-19 Premier League season!

KALIDOU
KOULIBALY

Centre-back

Club: Napoli

DOB: 20/06/1991

Place of Birth:
Saint-Die-des-Vosges, France

Transfer Value: £95 million

Strongest Foot: Right

Country: Senegal

International Debut:
05/09/2015 v Namibia

International Caps: 38

International Goals: 0

Top Skill: Monster power

Ranked as one of the best ball-playing defenders around, at over six feet tall Kalidou Koulibaly is a giant of a player. He's mega strong in the tackle, reads the game well and brings the ball out of defence with the kind of pace not expected of such a big guy. His passing is top notch too and he's pretty handy in the air. After first developing his skills in the French and Belgian leagues, he was signed by Italian club Napoli and he hasn't looked back since. In his first five seasons in Italy, he helped the team finish as Serie A runners-up three times and was a key member of the side that pushed Juventus hard in the title race in 2017-18. Ever since then, he's been linked with a move to many of the big clubs of Euro footy, so it won't be long before someone stumps up the cash to match his hefty price tag and make him the most expensive defender ever.

HIS GAME RATED!

 He drives out of defence and launches attacks with his perfect passing!

 He's mega tall and can be very strong and physical in the air!

 He's a big man and sometimes he gives too many fouls away!

PLAYER STATS

PACE
75

POWER
91

SHOOTING
50

DEFENDING
92

HEADERS
85

SKILL
69

DID YOU KNOW?

He played for France at the Under-20 World Cup before deciding to represent Senegal as a senior instead!

STAT ATTACK!

1

He won the Belgian Cup once in his two seasons playing for Genk!

4

He was included in the Serie A Team of the Year four times in his first five seasons in the Italian league!

11

The most yellow cards he's been given in a league season is 11 when playing for Napoli in 2015-16!

2

He's been voted Senegal's Player of the Year twice!

10

In his first five seasons in Serie A, he scored 10 goals for Napoli. His best season was 2017-18 when he scored five!

AYMERIC LAPORTE

Centre-back

Club: Manchester City
DOB: 27/05/1994
Place of Birth: Agen, France
Transfer Value: £62 million
Strongest Foot: Left

Country: France
International Debut: he has yet to make his senior debut
International Caps: 0
International Goals: 0
Top Skill: Footy brain

Aymeric Laporte has been the rock at the heart of Man. City's defence since he transferred to the Etihad Stadium for a club record fee in January 2018. So much so, that when injury ruled him out of a huge chunk of the 2019-20 season, his absence dented City's chances of winning a third Prem title in a row. It was like they just couldn't cope without him. That's why Pep Guardiola has called him the best left-sided central defender in

Europe. In his first two seasons at City, he added a ton of silverware to the Spanish Super Cup that he won with Athletic Bilbao. But despite his wicked success in club footy, his international experience has been limited. He represented France at youth level and captained the Under-19s to second place in the 2013 Euros, but he still hasn't won a cap for the seniors despite being called-up to the squad several times. They must be mad!

HIS GAME RATED!

 He's happy with the ball at his feet and he loves to pass!

 He's cool under pressure and doesn't dive in to tackles!

 He's not the fastest defender out of the blocks!

PLAYER STATS

PACE
68

POWER
86

SHOOTING
50

DEFENDING
89

HEADERS
85

SKILL
72

STAT ATTACK!

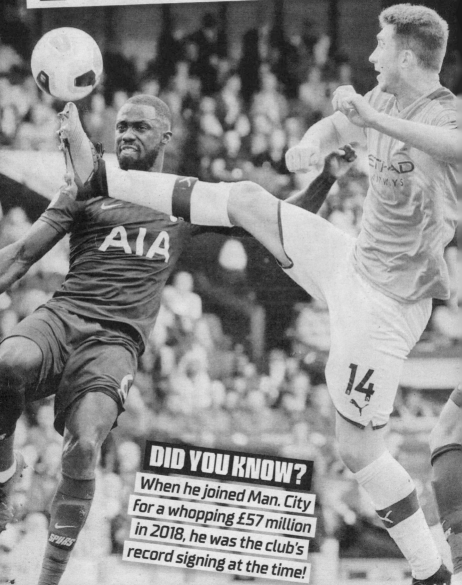

DID YOU KNOW?
When he joined Man. City for a whopping £57 million in 2018, he was the club's record signing at the time!

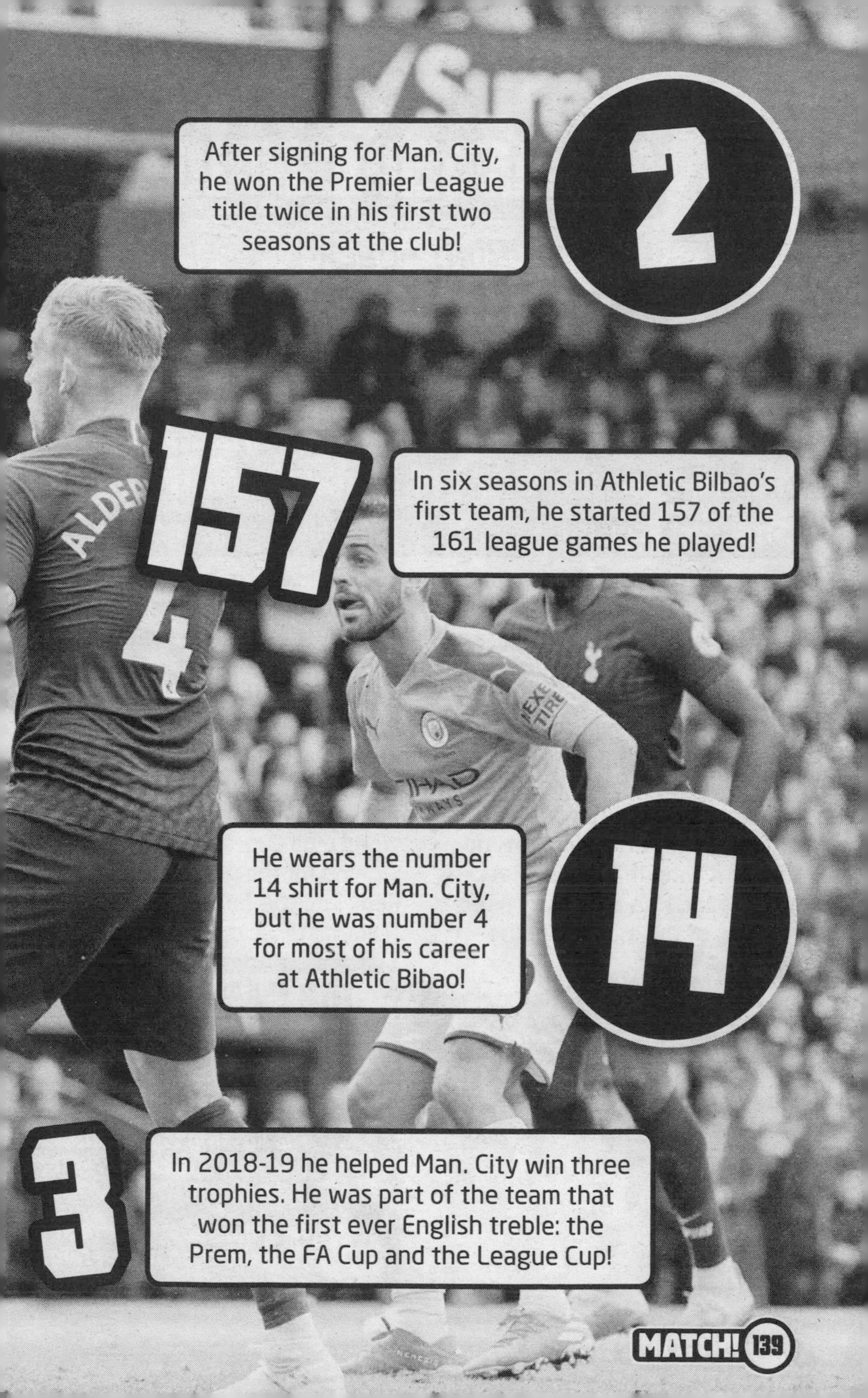

2

After signing for Man. City, he won the Premier League title twice in his first two seasons at the club!

157

In six seasons in Athletic Bilbao's first team, he started 157 of the 161 league games he played!

14

He wears the number 14 shirt for Man. City, but he was number 4 for most of his career at Athletic Bibao!

3

In 2018-19 he helped Man. City win three trophies. He was part of the team that won the first ever English treble: the Prem, the FA Cup and the League Cup!

TRENT
ALEXANDER-ARNOLD

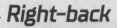

Right-back

Club: Liverpool	**Country:** England
DOB: 07/10/1998	**International Debut:** 07/06/2018 v Costa Rica
Place of Birth: Liverpool, England	**International Caps:** 9
Transfer Value: £95 million	**International Goals:** 1
Strongest Foot: Right	**Top Skill:** Set-pieces

Trent is Liverpool through and through, having joined the club when he was just six. Now he's played over 100 games for the first team and has set a record as the youngest ever player to appear in consecutive Champions League finals. Although he's a defender, he's become more famous at Anfield for his attacking runs up the right wing than for his tackling at the back. He's even built a rep as the king of the assists – in the 2018-19 season, he finished an amazing third in the Prem's assists charts. He also made headlines with his wicked, quickly-taken corner that set up Divock Origi to score the goal that knocked Barcelona out of the Champions League and put Liverpool into the final. He was at it again in the 2019 World Club Cup, setting up Bobby Firmino for the goal that put the Reds into the final. No wonder his team-mates love him!

HIS GAME RATED!

 He likes to bomb up the wing on overlapping attacking runs!

 His passing is first rate and he's a wicked crosser of the ball!

 He's much better at going forward than recovering to defend!

PLAYER STATS

PACE
84

POWER
76

SHOOTING
67

DEFENDING
85

HEADERS
70

SKILL
82

MATCH! 141

DID YOU KNOW?

He's enjoyed playing chess ever since his dad taught him the game when he was a kid!

STAT ATTACK!

12 His 12 assists in 2018-19 set a new Premier League record for the most assists by a defender in a season!

He doesn't score many goals, but in 10 games for England Under-19s he netted six times. It should have been seven but one was later put down as an opposition own goal!

14 In the 2018-19 season, he committed just 14 fouls in 29 Premier League games!

His shirt number has always been 66 when playing for the Liverpool first team!

5 He scored his first England goal in just his fifth game for his country, when he blasted the ball into the net against the USA at Wembley in 2018!

MATTHIJS DE LIGT

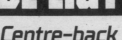

Centre-back

Club: Juventus

DOB: 12/08/1999

Place of Birth: Leiderdorp, Netherlands

Transfer Value: £67 million

Strongest Foot: Right

Country: Netherlands

International Debut: 25/03/2017 v Bulgaria

International Caps: 23

International Goals: 2

Top Skill: Passing

Tall, strong and impressive on the ball, Matthijs is an amazing footy prospect. By the age of 17, he had already broken into the Ajax team and played his first game for the Netherlands. He'd also become the youngest player in a major Euro final when facing Man. United in the 2017 Europa League decider. The following year, he became the first defender to receive the Golden Boy award, given each year to the best young player in Europe. As previous winners have included Rooney, Messi, Pogba and Mbappe, he's definitely in good company! Still only 19, he joined Italian giants Juventus in a mega bucks transfer in 2019 and his highlights have included scoring his first goal for the club in the local derby against city rivals Torino. But it's not all been gravy – his international debut was ruined by a couple of costly mistakes and it's taken him some time to settle into the team at Juve.

HIS GAME RATED!

✓ He's calm in possession and it's rare for him to lose the ball!

✓ He's great in the air, both when attacking and defending!

✗ He can sometimes make rash decisions and slide into risky tackles!

PACE
72

POWER
85

SHOOTING
65

DEFENDING
88

HEADERS
87

SKILL
73

STAT ATTACK!

DID YOU KNOW?
He was red carded in just his second international for the Netherlands!

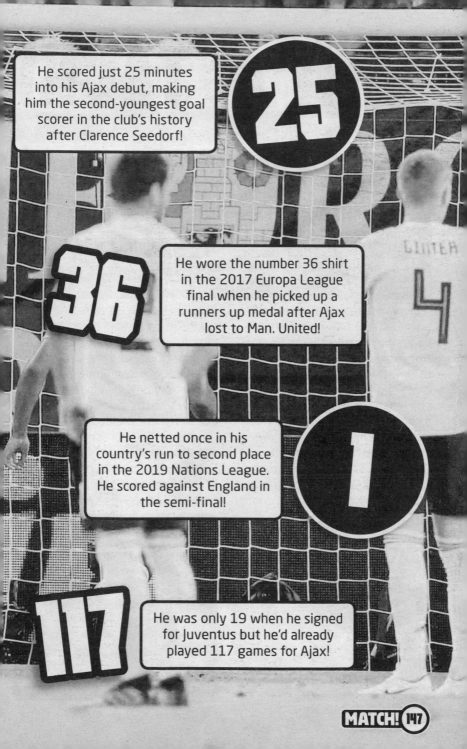

25

He scored just 25 minutes into his Ajax debut, making him the second-youngest goal scorer in the club's history after Clarence Seedorf!

36

He wore the number 36 shirt in the 2017 Europa League final when he picked up a runners up medal after Ajax lost to Man. United!

1

He netted once in his country's run to second place in the 2019 Nations League. He scored against England in the semi-final!

117

He was only 19 when he signed for Juventus but he'd already played 117 games for Ajax!

ALISSON

Goalkeeper

Club: Liverpool	**Country:** Brazil
DOB: 02/10/1992	**International Debut:** 13/10/2015 v Venezuela
Place of Birth: Novo Hamburgo, Brazil	**International Caps:** 44
Transfer Value: £78 million	**International Goals:** 0
Strongest Foot: Right	**Top Skill:** Shot-stopping

Liverpool destroyed the world transfer record for a goalkeeper when they signed Alisson Becker from Roma in 2018, but he proved to be just what the Reds needed to challenge for major honours. It all started off so differently though, as he made a horrendous blunder to concede his first ever Premier League goal. His attempt at a Cruyff turn went horribly wrong and allowed Leicester to nip in and score, but he was confident enough to bounce back. He ended his debut campaign at Anfield by getting his oversized mitts on the Champions League trophy and he even added the Prem's Golden Glove award to the honour he'd won in Italy as Serie A's best keeper. And it just got better for the beardy Brazilian, because in 2019 he smashed it at the Copa America as Brazil became South American champs and he finished the year by winning the Club World Cup with Liverpool!

HIS GAME RATED!

 He has great reflexes and he's a wicked shot-stopper!

 He's very quick to race off his line to stop an incoming attack!

 He's not really at his best when coming to meet crosses!

PLAYER STATS

REFLEXES
90

SHOT-STOP
93

AGILITY
87

CATCHING
86

KICKING
90

PEN. SAVES
89

DID YOU KNOW?
Alisson's older brother Muriel is also a top keeper!

STAT ATTACK!

17

In his one season of Serie A football with Roma, he kept 17 clean sheets in 37 games, saving two of the five pens he faced!

When he won the Prem's Golden Glove award in 2018-19, he kept 21 clean sheets from 38 games. That was one more than his Brazil team-mate Ederson achieved at Man. City!

21

1,170

In Liverpool's Champions League winning campaign of 2018-19, he played every minute of all 13 games. That 1,170 minutes in total!

It might be unlucky for some but when Liverpool won the Champions League in 2019, Alisson was wearing the number 13 shirt!

13

1

He helped Brazil to win the 2019 Copa America by only conceding one goal in six games at the finals!

FIRST XI!

Can you answer these 11 tough footy questions?

1. How many times has Sergio Ramos won the Champions League - three, four or five?

2. Who was Andy Robertson playing for when he made his Premier League debut?

3. Which German club did Marc-Andre ter Stegen play for before signing for Barcelona?

4. Which country did Matthijs de Ligt make his international debut against - Bulgaria or Belarus?

5. How many goals did Brazil keeper Alisson concede at the 2019 Copa America finals – one, three or five?

6. Which defender was voted Premier League Player of the Season for 2018-19?

7. What country did Kalidou Koulibaly represent at youth level before changing to Senegal?

8. Which top Man. City defender won the Spanish Super Cup with Athletic Bilbao in 2015?

9. What is Trent Alexander-Arnold's shirt number for Liverpool – No.2 or No.66?

10. Which current defender is Spain's most capped player?

11. Virgil van Dijk scored on his Liverpool debut but who was it against – Everton or Arsenal?

SOCCER SCRAMBLE

Use the remaining letters to discover the top goalkeeper!

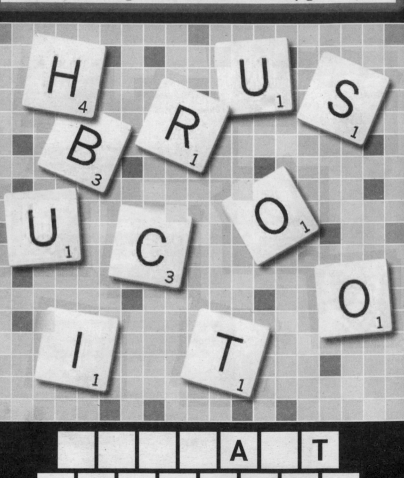

| | | | | A | | T |
| | | | T | | I | |

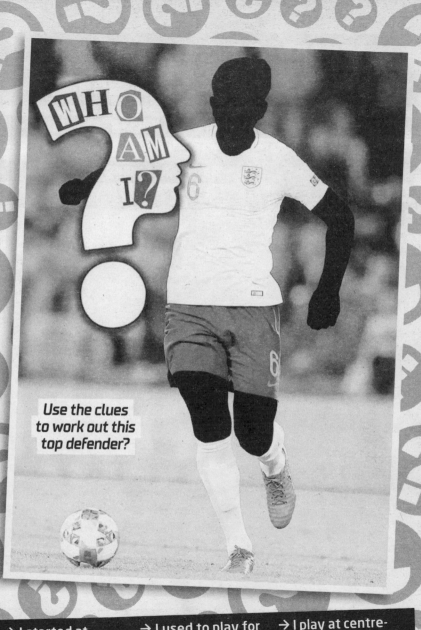

WHO AM I?

Use the clues to work out this top defender?

→ I started at Sheffield United!

→ I used to play for Hull and Leicester!

→ I play at centre-back for England!

QUIZ ANSWERS!

FIRST XI

1. Four
2. Hull City
3. Monchengladbach
4. Bulgaria
5. One
6. Virgil van Dijk
7. France
8. Aymeric Laporte
9. No.66
10. Sergio Ramos
11. Everton

SOCCER SCRAMBLE

Thibaut Courtois

WHO AM I?

Harry Maguire

WOMEN

LUCY BRONZE

Right-back

Club: Lyon	**Country:** England
DOB: 28/10/1991	**International Debut:** 26/06/2013 v Japan
Place of Birth: Berwick-upon-Tweed, England	**International Caps:** 79
Strongest Foot: Right	**International Goals:** 8

Easily the biggest star of the England team, Lucy Bronze is the most awesome of the Lionesses! She's best known as a right-back but she's so good that she can play almost anywhere in defence or midfield. After a series of mega performances at the 2019 World Cup and a memorable wonder goal against Norway, she collected the Silver Ball as the tourno's second-best player. Later in the year, she became the first English footballer and the first defender to win the UEFA Women's Player of the Year award and she also made it to third in the FIFA Player of the Year list. Her record in club footy has been no less impressive. After clinching the Women's Super League title and the FA Cup with Man. City, the tough defender earned a big move to Lyon, where she won back-to-back Champions Leagues. She also claimed two French league titles and the French Cup. She's going to need a bigger trophy cabinet soon!

HER GAME RATED!

 She's great at driving forward with the ball at her feet!

✓ *Her tackling is wicked and she's a really physical player!*

 To be the best she really needs a World Cup winners' medal!

PLAYER STATS

PACE
87

POWER
85

SHOOTING
70

DEFENDING
91

HEADERS
86

SKILL
83

STAT ATTACK!

14

In each of her two seasons at Liverpool, she played 14 Women's Super League games. That's every game of the season!

DID YOU KNOW?

Her full name is Lucia Roberta Tough Bronze – but her team mates call her 'Bronzey'!

5

She scored five WSL goals for Man. City in her three seasons with the club!

87

When she won her first French league title in the 2017-18 season, she spent 1,655 minutes on the pitch. That's an average of 87 minutes per game!

42

During the 2019 Women's World Cup, she covered 42 miles while playing seven games!

SAM KERR

Forward

Club: Chelsea	**Country:** Australia
DOB: 10/09/1993	**International Debut:** 07/02/2009 v Italy
Place of Birth: East Freemantle, Australia	**International Caps:** 83
Strongest Foot: Right	**International Goals:** 38

Australian soccer superstar Sam Kerr is one of the best strikers in the world and she became the biggest name to play in the English WSL when she made her debut for Chelsea in January 2020. She can create something from nothing on the pitch and she's shown herself to be an out and out goal scorer for both club and country. She's got loads of skills, the pace to beat defenders and she can score in so many ways – she's great with her right foot, good with her left and is powerful in the air, having modelled her heading style on men's Aussie footy legend, Tim Cahill. She's so red hot in the penalty box that she managed to win five Golden Boots in a row, three in the American NWSL and two in the Australian W-League, and she's the all-time top scorer in both. She's the captain of her country too and in 2019 she became the first Australian player, man or woman, to score a hat-trick at a World Cup. That makes this Matilda, a super Aussie!

HER GAME RATED!

✓ She's not the tallest player but she's still stupidly good in the air!

✓ She does a pretty wicked backflip goal celebration after scoring!

✗ She has a bit of a hit and miss record from the penalty spot!

PACE
90

POWER
84

SHOOTING
93

DEFENDING
51

HEADERS
92

SKILL
89

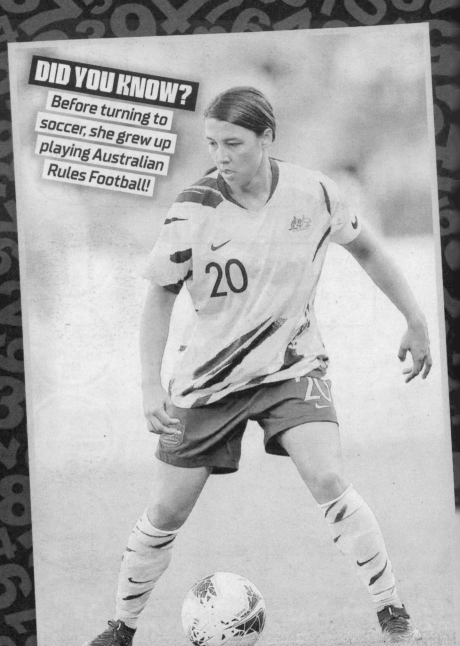

DID YOU KNOW?

Before turning to soccer, she grew up playing Australian Rules Football!!

STAT ATTACK!

77 She has scored 77 goals in the National Women's Soccer League in America, making her the league's all-time top scorer!

In an amazing run of form in the second half of 2017, she scored 11 international goals in just six games!

3 In her time playing in the USA she won the National Women's Soccer League Golden Boot three times in a row!

In two seasons with Chicago Red Stars she scored 34 goals in 40 league games!

4 At the 2019 World Cup she bagged all four of Australia's goals against Jamaica. That's the most goals she's scored in a single international match!

ALEX MORGAN

Striker

Club: Orlando Pride	**Country:** USA
DOB: 02/07/1989	**International Debut:** 31/03/2010 v Mexico
Place of Birth: San Dimas, USA	**International Caps:** 169
Strongest Foot: Left	**International Goals:** 107

Alex Morgan is one of the deadliest strikers in women's football, but the Orlando Pride star also has one of the weirdest nicknames. She was called 'Baby Horse' by her international team mates when she was first called up to the USA squad, due to her galloping running style, and the name has hung about ever since. A fast and athletic striker, she's really comfortable with the ball at her feet and is known for her direct style of play. She's a double World Cup winner and an Olympic gold medallist with the USA, but although she has spent almost all of her club career playing in her home country, in 2017 she spent six months on loan to Lyon. In that spell she managed to win both the French league title and the Champions League. Two years later, she became only the second player to score five times in a Women's World Cup game, bagging her goals in a 13-0 crushing of Thailand. That's pretty good going!

HER GAME RATED!

 Defenders struggle to keep up with her powerful running!

 She's a sick dribbler and loves to go one-on-one with opponents!

 As she's got older, she's picked up injuries and that's affected her game!

PLAYER STATS

PACE
89

POWER
79

SHOOTING
87

DEFENDING
54

HEADERS
85

SKILL
87

STAT ATTACK!

In 2012 she racked up 28 goals and 21 assists in 31 USA games. She was only the second American woman to achieve 20 goals and 20 assists in the same year!

Between her international debut in 2010 and the end of 2019, she scored 107 times for the USA. That's an awesome decade of goals!

The five goals she bagged against Thailand at the 2019 World Cup included her fifth international hat-trick!

DID YOU KNOW?

She made her acting debut playing herself in the 2018 comedy film 'Alex & Me'!

6

Of her six goals at the 2019 World Cup, she scored three with her left foot, one with her right and two with her head!

VIVIANNE MIEDEMA

Forward

Club: Arsenal	**Country:** Netherlands
DOB: 15/07/1996	**International Debut:** 26/09/2013 v Albania
Place of Birth: Hoogeveen, Netherlands	**International Caps:** 87
Strongest Foot: Right	**International Goals:** 69

Vivianne Miedema has a knack for scoring goals. Her team mates say all they need to do is feed the ball to her in the penalty area and she'll find the back of the net. Still young, by the time she turned 23 she had already won the German league twice with Bayern Munich. She'd also helped Arsenal lift the FA Cup and win a first WSL title in seven years. However, none of this compares to her achievements for the Netherlands. She played a big part in a shock triumph at Euro 2017, when her two goals in the final put the Dutch on course to become the best on the continent. Two years later she picked up a World Cup runners-up medal and became her country's all-time top scorer. Back at Arsenal after the World Cup, she bagged six goals and set up four more in just one game, helping the Gunners crush Bristol City by a record 11-1 tally. That's not too shoddy for a player who doesn't believe in celebrating when she scores!

HER GAME RATED!

 Great with both feet, she's more than just a goal poacher!

 She works hard off the ball to make space for her team-mates!

❌ *Her only real football weakness is her lack of pace!*

PACE
77

POWER
87

SHOOTING
90

DEFENDING
51

HEADERS
84

SKILL
87

DID YOU KNOW?

Growing up as a Feyenoord fan, her footy hero was Dutch legend Robin van Persie!

STAT ATTACK!

In 2013-14 she finished the season as the BeNe League's top scorer with 39 goals in 26 games for Heerenveen!

Her goals fired the Netherlands to the World Cup for the first time in 2015. She finished as the top goal scorer in the qualifying campaign with 16!

3

In the 2015-16 season only six hat-tricks were scored in the German Bundesliga but three of them were scored for Bayern Munich by Viv!

During the 2019 World Cup she covered 40 miles in seven games!

She broke the record for most goals in an English WSL season in 2018-19, netting 22 times!

MARTA

Forward

Club: Orlando Pride

DOB: 19/02/1986

Place of Birth:
Dois Riachos, Brazil

Strongest Foot: Left

Country: Brazil

International Debut:
19/11/2002

International Caps: 151

International Goals: 107

Once the greatest star of women's football, Marta may have been voted the best player in the world six times, but she still hasn't won the biggest trophy on the planet. Like Lionel Messi with Argentina, Marta's solo skill has not been enough to lead Brazil to World Cup glory. A second-place finish in 2007 is the closest she's come, while Olympic gold medals have slipped through her hands twice when Brazil picked up silver. In club footy, she's got a trophy cabinet stuffed with silverware and has won the UEFA Women's Cup (now the Champions League) with Swedish side Umea. She also won the American regular season league title three times with Los Angeles Sol, Gold Pride and Western New York Flash, and the Swedish league title seven times with Umea, Rosengard and Tyreso. In South America, she won the Copa Libertadores with Santos in 2009 and was voted best player in the comp. That's pretty good going!

HER GAME RATED!

✓ Her quick feet and creativity make her tough to play against!

✓ She's hard to stop when she dribbles at defenders with speed!

✗ She's getting older and is no longer the player she once was!

PLAYER STATS

PACE
89

POWER
71

SHOOTING
87

DEFENDING
50

HEADERS
79

SKILL
92

STAT ATTACK!

She scored seven goals at the 2007 World Cup, which was enough to win her the Golden Boot as the top scorer and the Golden Ball as the best player!

 She has two Olympic silver medals after Brazil finished runners-up in 2004 and 2008!

Having played in five World Cup tournaments, she holds the all-time scoring record with 17 goals!

She has been voted the best women's player in the world six times. That's more than any other player!

DID YOU KNOW?
She left home at 14, taking a three-day bus journey across Brazil to join her first club, Vasco da Gama!

ADA HEGERBERG

Striker

Club: Lyon	**Country:** Norway
DOB: 10/07/1995	**International Debut:** 19/11/2011 v Northern Ireland
Place of Birth: Molde, Norway	**International Caps:** 66
Strongest Foot: Right	**International Goals:** 38

Ada Hegerberg made her top-flight debut in Norway aged just 15. Since then she has racked up more than 300 goals for club and country – and she's still only in her mid 20s. An awesome footballer, in 2016 she was voted UEFA Best Women's Player in Europe. Two years later she became the first winner of the Women's Ballon d'Or. The only reason she's not currently ranked higher is that she was the biggest star missing from the 2019 Women's World Cup. This was due to her public falling out with the Norwegian FA, but she's more than made up for it in club footy. Since 2014 she's been a key member of the all-conquering Lyon team. In her first five seasons with the club, she won the Champions League four times. She even clinched the 2019 final with a 16-minute hat-trick against Barcelona. In the same five-year period, she also won the French league five times and finished as its top scorer on three occasions. Stunning stats!

HER GAME RATED!

✓ An out and out number nine, she has a great eye for goal!

✓ She's a skilful dribbler and likes to power forward with the ball!

✗ Her absence from international footy has been a big let down!

PLAYER STATS

PACE
82

POWER
80

SHOOTING
86

DEFENDING
51

HEADERS
90

SKILL
91

DID YOU KNOW?

Ada's older sister Andrine Hegerberg is also footballer and has played for Norway!

STAT ATTACK!

4

She picked up four Champions League winners' medals in her first five seasons at Lyon, scoring five times in the final!

Up to the end of 2019 she had scored 53 goals in the Champions League, making her the competition's all-time top scorer!

53

130

In her first five seasons at Lyon, she scored 130 league goals in just 105 games!

In the 2017-18 season she scored 15 Champions League goals, averaging one every 54 minutes in Lyon's run to the trophy!

15

3

She scored a hat-trick in the 2019 Champions League Final as Lyon beat Barcelona 4-1!

MEGAN RAPINOE

Winger

Club: Reign

DOB: 05/07/1985

Place of Birth: Redding, USA

Strongest Foot: Right

Country: USA

International Debut: 23/07/2006 v Rep. of Ireland

International Caps: 165

International Goals: 51

Megan Rapinoe became the most famous women's footballer on the planet in 2019 – and not just because of her shocking pink hair. Up until the World Cup, she'd had a pretty quiet year, but her wicked performances for the USA turned her into a superstar. Not only was she voted Player of the Match for her role in the World Cup final, but she was judged to be the tourno's best player and she finished its top scorer too. Her goal celebration after scoring in the quarters against the hosts became the most iconic image of the competition and soon afterwards she was crowned FIFA's Women's Player of the Year. In her mid 30s, she isn't just a legend for starring at France 2019, she's had a great career too. She's won two World Cups and Olympic gold with the USA, while in club footy she's clinched the French league with Lyon and is a two-time winner of America's regular season league title with Seattle Reign. Let's just call her 'Mega Megan'!

HER GAME RATED!

 She's a sick dribbler and loves to go one-on-one with defenders!

 Strong on the ball, even under pressure her hold up play is fantastic!

Injuries have robbed her of some of her pace and acceleration!

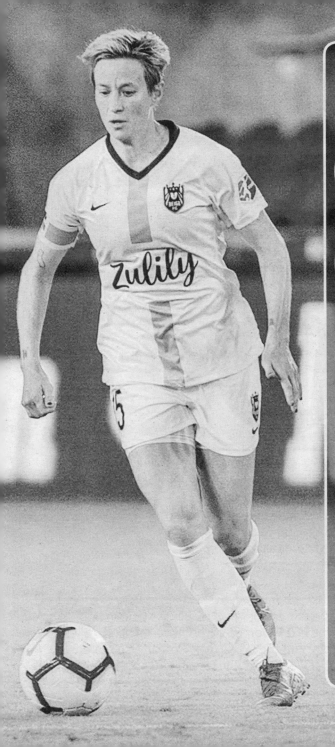

PACE
79

POWER
72

SHOOTING
82

DEFENDING
51

HEADERS
79

SKILL
93

STAT ATTACK!

50

Rapinoe's penalty in the 2019 World Cup Final was her 50th international goal, scored in her 158th game for her country!

16

She took 16 corners at the 2019 Women's World Cup - that makes her the top USA corner taker at the tournament!

6

She scored six goals to win the Golden Boot at the 2019 Women's World Cup. England's Ellen White and the USA's Alex Morgan also scored six, but Megan did it in less minutes on the pitch!

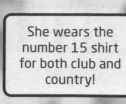
She wears the number 15 shirt for both club and country!

15

DID YOU KNOW?

In 2012 she became the first player, male or female, to score a goal directly from a corner at the Olympic Games!

ELLEN WHITE

Striker

Club: Manchester City

DOB: 09/05/1989

Place of Birth: Aylesbury, England

Strongest Foot: Right

Country: England

International Debut: 25/03/2010 v Austria

International Caps: 89

International Goals: 35

England fans loved Ellen White's famous goal celebration at the 2019 Women's World Cup. They got to see plenty of it too, as she netted six times during the tourno. A ruthless finisher with a knack for getting herself in the right place at the right time, she's been one of the mega stars of the Lionesses since she lobbed the Japan keeper from 20 yards to score an awesome wonder goal at the 2011 World Cup. She's been a hit in club footy too. She scored twice for Leeds against Everton in the 2010 League Cup final to lift the trophy, and she won the league title and the Women's FA Cup twice each with Arsenal, scoring for the Gunners in the 2013 final. During a spell at Birmingham City she finished the 2017-18 season as the top goal scorer in the WSL and shortly before the 2019 World Cup, her goal scoring reputation was further recognised when she was signed to lead the line for title contenders Man. City. What a star!

HER GAME RATED!

 She's a strong and physical presence in the penalty area!

 She presses quick and high to regain the ball when possession is lost!

✗ She lacks pace but the quality of her finishing makes up for this!

PACE
70

POWER
88

SHOOTING
85

DEFENDING
58

HEADERS
88

SKILL
79

DID YOU KNOW?

Her famous 'goggles' goal celebration at the 2019 World Cup was borrowed from Koln striker Anthony Modeste!

STAT ATTACK!

4

Although she plays her international footy for England, she represented Great Britain four times at the 2012 Olympics!

She scored 15 league goals for Birmingham City in the 2017-18 season when she won the WSL Golden Boot!

15

6

Ellen was joint top scorer at the 2019 World Cup with six goals but finished third in the race for the Golden Boot after assists and pitch-time were taken into account!

She has been voted England Women's Player of the Year twice. She won the award in 2011 and 2018!

2

36

In six matches at the 2019 World Cup, she covered 36 miles on the pitch!

ROSE LAVELLE

Midfielder

Club: Washington Spirit

DOB: 14/05/1995

Place of Birth: Cincinnati, USA

Strongest Foot: Left

Country: USA

International Debut: 04/03/2017 v England

International Caps: 42

International Goals: 12

The brightest young star of the US soccer team, Lavelle dazzled fans with her wicked skills and darting runs at the 2019 World Cup and she gave even the most stubborn defenders the toughest of times. She scored three goals on the way to collecting her winners' medal and was so impressive that she was awarded the Bronze Ball as one of the tourno's best players. In fact, she was ranked an amazing third behind Megan Rapinoe and Lucy Bronze. In the World Cup final itself, her driving run to the edge of the box and the smashing shot that followed was one of the standout goals of the comp. She's obviously comfortable in big games, because she also scored the opener in the final of the 2018 CONCACAF Women's Championship. She's so skilful, she's even been compared to some of the legends of the men's game, such as Leo Messi and Zinedine Zidane. That's not a bad shout, as she's tipped to be a future legend of the game herself!

HER GAME RATED!

 Blessed with magic feet, she's known for her awesome skills!

 She's nicknamed the 'Nutmeg Duchess' for her ability to panna!

✗ *She's often the shortest on the pitch and she lacks physical strength!*

GEICO

PLAYER STATS

PACE
83

POWER
60

SHOOTING
77

DEFENDING
50

HEADERS
51

SKILL
88

STAT ATTACK!

She wore the number 16 shirt for the USA at the 2019 World Cup!

She scored three goals at the 2018 CONCACAF Women's Championship – that's the equivalent to the Euros for North America, Central America and the Caribbean!

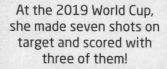

At the 2019 World Cup, she made seven shots on target and scored with three of them!

She was voted sixth best women's player in the world at the Best FIFA Football Awards in 2019!

DID YOU KNOW?

She loves dogs and is very proud of her English bulldog, which she named Wilma Jean Wrinkles!

WENDIE RENARD

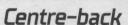

Centre-back

Club: Lyon	**Country:** France
DOB: 20/07/1990	**International Debut:** 02/03/2011 v Switzerland
Place of Birth: Schoelcher, Martinique	**International Caps:** 118
Strongest Foot: Right	**International Goals:** 23

Growing up on the Caribbean island of Martinique, Wendie Renard moved to France to play footy for Lyon when she was just 16 and she's been at the club ever since. One of the most decorated players in the game, she is the long-standing captain of Lyon, who are by far the most successful women's team in Europe. By the end of the 2018-19 season, she'd won the Champions League six times with the club, plus an amazing 13 straight French league titles. That's a pretty sick medal haul! A tall and strong central defender, her style of play has been compared to that of Virgil van Dijk. Like the Liverpool star, she's always amazingly calm under pressure at the back and at ease on the ball when going forward. She can score more than her share of goals too, often using her height to good advantage. In fact, she bagged four at the World Cup in 2019, making her France's top scorer at the tournament. Not bad going for a defender!

HER GAME RATED!

✓ She's a physical centre-back, but she's good with the ball at her feet too!

✓ She's really powerful in the air and great at heading clear!

✗ An own goal at the World Cup showed that even legends have an off day!

PLAYER STATS

PACE
71

POWER
95

SHOOTING
87

DEFENDING
92

HEADERS
96

SKILL
75

DID YOU KNOW?

When she was young, she was inspired to play footy by watching Brazil legend Ronaldinho on the telly!

STAT ATTACK!

3

She wears the number 3 shirt for both club and country!

In her first 13 seasons with Lyon, Renard managed to win an amazing 13 French league titles!

13

213

Up until the end of the 2018-19 season she had played 213 league games for Lyon!

By 2019 she had won the Women's Champions League with Lyon six times – four of them as captain!

6

187

Standing at 187cm, Wendie Renard was the tallest player at the 2019 Women's World Cup.

FIRST XI!

Can you answer these 11 tough footy questions?

1. Who won the Golden Boot at the 2019 FIFA Women's World Cup – Rapinoe or Lavelle?

2. Can you name the Australian forward who made her debut for Chelsea in January 2020?

3. Alex Morgan scored five goals in a single World Cup game in 2019. Who was it against?

4. Which team was Ellen White playing for when she won the WSL Golden Boot in 2017-18?

5. Which country both hosted and won the 2017 UEFA Women's European Championship?

6. Which England player won the Silver Ball at the 2019 FIFA Women's World Cup?

7. Marta holds the all-time scoring record at the Women's World Cup. How many goals has she scored?

8. Can you name the lethal USA striker nicknamed 'Baby Horse' by her team-mates?

9. Who scored a hat-trick in the 2019 UEFA Women's Champions League Final – Hegerberg or Kerr?

10. How many goals did France defender Wendie Renard score at the 2019 Women's World Cup?

11. Who scored six goals in one WSL game for Arsenal in the 2019-20 season?

WORDSEARCH

Can you find the 20 top players from the women's game?

Bardsley	Bronze ✓
Ertz	Hansen
Hegerberg	Henry
Houghton	Jakobsson
Kerr	Lavelle

Marta	Miedema
Morgan	Rapinoe
Renard	Scott
Seger	Spitse
Van Veenendaal	White ✓

 200 MATCH!

```
Y K Q S X K A A A T R A M X A R W N L
L C R W Y A G Y R Y N K E X W R J O I
G A U N W I X N B P E F C L K E J S O
P F D V F E Y A L M S I Z H B K U S G
M G H H W R C S M E N P T Z E G I B Y
S Z V A M E D E I M A D I Y L X P O N
Q S J D N W V V F W H F R E L O C K R
Q K R D T S U C H C T S K L E B T A I
F H Z K N K Q A G D E P T S V X F J Z
K K U R E L A Q H Q V I D D A F E P K
K E R T Q N A G R O M T R R L S Y K E
H P Z R L P P G T Q B S L A J L T T D
X R A P I N O E T U D E X B W S I H I
W X I O P V A N V E E N E N D A A L M
K O S M J J T H V H Q O K V L K N F B
N P Z R Z H Y C O F D N R H E U I Q R
F F F Y Z H E O J U R E D D J Q V I O
R V C D J E Y G Q L G I P Y R T X E N
V I O M X N K J E J F H Q O B T T D Z
G T Y L N R B E Z R Y W T L O O V C E
R T L I C Y V A I V B G F O D C M V H
E B S B J Y W L S Z Z E I B N S I L D
N W U H Y W T E N T C C R X T E A P J
A W Q C M V G Q R D X L D G T W H R P
R T T T Z E T O Y B D R E T D H L F J
D F V P R X B H F B S I U I Y W E C K
L F L D D D L A Y Y N L M V M E R R W
I L H L Y G S Q X U B H S A U K T U I
W H I T E M G O S D S S M G Q A Z P A
```

QUIZ ANSWERS!

FIRST XI

1. Megan Rapinoe
2. Sam Kerr
3. Thailand
4. Birmingham City
5. Netherlands
6. Lucy Bronze
7. 17
8. Alex Morgan
9. Ada Hegerberg
10. Four
11. Vivianne Miedema

WORDSEARCH

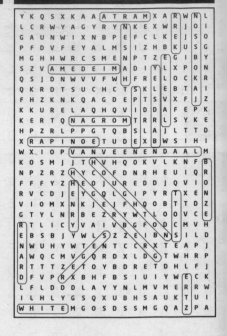

MY TOP 10

Pick your top 10 footballers from the players in this book!

1

2

3

4

5

6

7

8

9

10

SUBSCRIPTION OFFER

LOVE MATCH?

PREMIER LEAGUE ADRENALYN XL TRADING CARDS!

2 PACKS OF ADRENALYN XL!

MATCH!

GIFTS! GIFTS! GIFTS! GIFTS! GIFTS! GIFTS! GIFTS! GIFTS!

14 SKILL KINGS POSTERS!

SKILLS SPECIAL! FOOTY'S TOP TRICKSTERS REVEALED!

INTERVIEWS! The FZ & The Knuckleball Twins

TOP TEKKERS!

BIG SAVINGS ON SHOP PRICES!

WONDERKID WATCH!

WIN! Nintendo Switch bundle

FA CUP QUARTERS!

GET IT DELIVERED EVERY WEEK!

EVERY WEEK YOU'LL GET . . .

★ Cool gear ★ FIFA tips ★ Stats & Facts
★ Top stars ★ Quizzes ★ Posters & more!

FREE DELIVERY TO YOUR DOOR!

IT'S SO EASY!

TRY FOUR ISSUES FOR JUST £1*

CHECK OUT OUR BEST DEALS!

CALL 📱
01959 543 747
QUOTE: MB20

ONLINE 🖱
shop.kelsey.co.uk/
MB20

*Discounted subscription offer may not include all covermount gifts that are included with retail copies. UK Direct Debit offer only, available until March 31, 2021. You will pay £1 for your first 4 issues. Your subscription will then continue every 3 months at a rate of £19.50. Discounts are calculated on the full cover price. For overseas and UK credit/debit card offers, please visit our website at shop.kelsey.co.uk. For digital subscriptions, please visit shop.kelsey.co.uk/MATCH. Calls will be charged at your local network rate. Order lines are open 8.30am-5.30pm, Monday-Friday. Full terms and conditions can be found at shop.kelsey.co.uk/terms. Here at Kelsey Publishing we take your privacy very seriously and will only use your personal information to administer your account and to provide the products and services you have requested from us. We will only contact you about our special offers via the preferences you will indicate when ordering and you can update these at any time by emailing subs@kelsey.co.uk or by calling us on 01959 543 747.

CHECK OUT THESE OTHER MATCH! TITLES FROM MACMILLAN!

NO.1 BEST-SELLER!

OFFICIALLY THE UK'S BEST-SELLING FOOTBALL ANNUAL!

MATCH! ANNUAL 2021

THE ONLY FOOTBALL ANNUAL YOU NEED!

www.matchfootball.co.uk

INSIDE! EURO 2020 ★ UK & IRELAND DREAM TEAM ★ QUIZZES ★ WOMEN'S WC SCRAPBOOK ★ RONALDO V MESSI ★

MATCH! ANNUAL OUT SEPTEMBER 2020

MATCH! PUZZLE BOOK

MATCH! FOOTBALL RECORDS BOOK

MATCH! JOKE BOOK

MATCH! FUN BOOK

MATCH! ENGLAND HEROES BOOK

TO ORDER, GO TO: WWW.PANMACMILLAN.COM